VISHITAO

THE MINDLESS MIND OF UNIVERSE READY TO HELP YOU

DR. REKHAA KALE

Made with ♥ on the Notion Press Platform
www.notionpress.com

Contents

Contents

Contents

Preface

VISHITaO is a method of healing events and persons with the help of energized energy field. Here, one first creates an energy field, then visualizes his desired event in it, and then energizes it with necessary delineations put on that field in the necessary order.

This is the only healing method where touching a patient is NOT AT ALL required.

The complete diagnosis and healing of a patient or event or situation or relationship happens here, just by a technique of distance healing done after a simple breathing method.

The first class of VISHITAO was conducted on 1.1.1996. Ever since that day, every year, on the 1st January, class of Vishitao is being conducted.

This simple method of healing has shifted many lives since 1996.

The best part of Vishitao is that it never produces any adverse results or supports any intention meant to harm anyone.

The energy field produces harmony and wellbeing in any area about which one is putting any intention.

Also, if the intention of sender is totally negative, and if the sender wants to harm anyone, then energy field gives indication to the sender that intention needs to be revised.

Only after the intention is revised and the intention is presented as beneficial & positive for the sender without mentioning any negative thing for any one, energy field starts working. So, we can say that this is an absolutely safe method that anyone can use without any risk of mistake and adverse or side effect.

VISHITAO

1. Vishitao Introduction
2. How I received Vishitao
3. Healing with Vishitao
4. Things possible with Vishitao
5. Stages of Vishitao

CHAPTER I

Vishitao Introduction

Vishi: universal **Tao**: mindless mind

Vishi is universal and **Tao** is mindless mind.

So **Vishitao** is **mindless mind of universe**. Vishitao healing is done with guidance of omnipotent, omnipresent and omniscient mindless mind of universe.

Generally when we heal we use our mind and our mind has limitations! When we heal, we receive the universal life force signals.

But though we receive these signals, we cannot always interpret them.

This is something we still need to learn! Vishitao healing method teaches this.

With Vishitao, we not only are able to heal faster but also can know the divine wish clearly.

This method of healing is used strictly without touch, but one may try the usual touch healing by using the Vishitao delineations.

CHAPTER II

How I received Vishitao:

I must say that VISHITAO is a result of many days' long meditations that I was doing since 1992.

I did not meditate specifically to achieve anything or so, but yes, I always wished that I should be in tune with divine will and the Universal will may use my existence for some service to humanity.

Since Octoberber 1995, I was seeing various figures and formations at random intervals.

I felt like noting down the figures as and when I would see them.

I was not even particular about where I was noting them down! It was just that something made me note them down on a piece of paper!

Then on 30th Dec. 1995 it so happened that on the afternoon when I was sharing this with some Reiki healers as well as my own kids, the delineations started falling into different groups.

This time I had realized that I had written down all the delineations on one single sheet of paper without realizing this at these various times when I was noting down them.

Then at night at about 12, when all had slept, I started writing about each delineations and its uses as if somebody is dictating me. I went on writing till 4.00 AM in the morning.

This time the whole classification of the delineations into basic, material, mental and spiritual level was complete with explanation.

When I finished writing all this, I heard a serine voice telling me that from 1st Jan, I must start giving this gift to some selected capable masters for serving the Humanity.

I was shocked on listening this, as, I was not even aware as to how I was going to activate these delinations in those whom I would be teaching them. But What I had heard, was a divine order and it had to be followed! So I decided to abide by the order I had received.

On 31st December 1995, when everyone was preparing for the New Year's party, I was running around for getting the matter I had written converted into proper DTP to make the notes ready for the class to be conducted on 1st Jan 1996!

When everything about Vishitao was ready, I started inviting the selected persons, for visiting my place for the Vishitao Class. In fact, even these names had flashed in the divine signalI had heard, I just followed it!

I conducted the class on 1st Jan 1996. I had made it quite clear that whatever I was teaching them was something I had just received. I also told them that the training was being done as per the divine order.

I had clearly told them that I had not tested the delineations yet; so all of us would test them before actually trusting them and trusting the method.

Testing the system and genuine report of results was the only energy exchange for that first class. This class had only a group of experienced Reiki teachers who were absolutely scientific minded people.

The reports were wonderful. This confirmed that the system is very useful. Then I started teaching it.

CHAPTER III

Healing with Vishitao:

Vishitao heals with highly empowered and energized energy field.

This energy field is generated by drawing the universal energies from the existence.

One can do it in a certain way by using a method that we will learn and initiation that we receive during the training workshop.

In this book of Vishitao, readers can find all the methods of using all vishitao tools and delinations very clearly.

Some readers may just read the book and try to use the delinations. They may get some results also! But remember when the readers do this, they can get just 20% of the actual results.

Also, at times, one may fine that trying to use and practice these methods without initiation, just by reading the book means creating an illusion of healing and in turn accepting the dark and harmful energies of patient, that we feel we are removing.

So, one must take care of taking a proper initiation from a properly qualified Vishitao Teacher before one starts using it in the full fledged manner in life.

In short, to practice Vishitao, a seeker must learn this method from a qualified Guru and receive a correct initiation to be able to practice as a healer.

Looking at the very first stage of this method, we can say that, generally anyone can create the energy field just by following the instructions from the book.

But after the Vishitao attunement the same energy field that we can draw starts becoming much more powerful.

We draw the energies and create the filed, and then we further empower it with the delineations as per one requirement.

When the energy field is duly charged, we send it to do the necessary work much more effectively than the other existing methods.

In this way we can heal physical ailments, psychological tensions, emotional problems, natural events, relationship issues, financial problems and many other things like this!

CHAPTER IV

Things possible with Vishitao:

Vishitao can be used practically for doing anything whatsoever!

Yet, it is necessary to state these things more categorically.

Let us list out a few major things that are possible with Vishitao:

1. Working on minds of people
2. Keeping our loved ones healthy.
3. Create events of our choice
4. Increasing or decreasing things
5. Increasing or decreasing temperature
6. Avoiding natural calamities
7. Maintaining the balanced climate
8. Preventing social unrest
9. Increasing avarage or speed of vehicle
10. Mend healthy relationships
11. Remove improper unhealthy relations

This means, we can not only heal the physical and mental ailments and disturbances with Vishitao, but also we can create the events on physical plane.

Such events can be like changing the temperature of atmosphere around us or increasing the average or speed of the vehicle in which we are travelling etc.

When we wish to mend some relationship, we can do so with the help of using Vishitao delineations.

If we wish to create some good natural events like bringing the rain in the rainy season, we can do so with the help of some Vishitao delineations.

If we wish to reduce social unrest, we can do so with some Vishitao delineations.

When we suspect some natural calamities, we can cancel them with the help of some of the Vishitao delineations.

To enhance our vision and spiritual growth we can use these Vishitao delineations.

That means, we can work on all the physical, mental and spiritual planes with this system.

CHAPTER V

Stages of Vishitao:

VISHITAO is taught in 9 stages. These are classified into healer stages, teacher i.e. Guru Stages and Grand Master, i.e. Maha Guru stage.

There are 4 stages of a healer.

Then there are 4 stages of Vishitao Guru training

Then there is 1 level of Maha Guru training.

The **basic** level enables us to send energy field to a person or event. Here we use two basic delineations.

The **Material** level enables us to energize the energy field further with delineations for material desires. This strengthens our heating.

The **mental** level enables us to heal more effectively by using the power of the mind as well as the power of the mind of the healed ones. That means mental level delineations help the patient build stronger will power and a greater desire to get well soon.

The **spiritual** level takes us a step ahead! Here we can heal with the support of the Divine Masters and the angels in the universe! The spiritual level delineations are drawn by the Master healer from spiritual plane to heal or create event we work on.

These stages of Vishitao can be learnt separately with the desired amount of gap between levels or they can be learned in continuation in a period of 3 / 4 days.

Generally students are advised to learn all four stages of Vishitao to practice it effectively. Yet, if one wants one may learn just basic or so. But a seeker must remember that just the basic level has its own limitations.

Basic is the first or elementary level.

Material level is the second or intermediate level.

Mental level is the third or advanced level.

Spiritual is fourth & final level of Healers training.

These levels have to be learned in the same order. When healers' training is complete we may practice **VISHITAO** for some time.

Once a healer completes the first 4 levels of Vishitao, he is ready to receive Vishitao Guru's training.

This again goes in 4 stages.

Level 5 is the **Basic Guru** level. Here one learns how to teach the basic level of Vishitao.

Level 6 is the **MaterialGuru** level. Here one learns how to teach the Material level of Vishitao.

Level 7 is the **MentalGuru** level. Here one learns how to teach the mental level of Vishitao.

Level 8 is the **SpiritualGuru** level. Here one learns how to teach the spiritual level of Vishitao.

In each of **Guru** under Training levels, the **Guru** under training has to organize, assist & watch minimum 10 training sessions of the level he is being trained for.

Here he must watch how the Maha Guru is teaching and understand the basic techniques of training various aspects of the syllabus.

He must also realise that each human being is a different individual and has different training needs.

He must also observe and understand how people with different personalities react to certain thoughts, attitudes, healing techniques and healing energies and how they are handled by the Maha Guru.

As the Guru under training is doing this the Maha Guru will train him about various more things he has to learn for effective training.

The duration of each level of Guru training and number of training sessions needed to be assisted in may be increased or decreased as per the readiness of Guru under training.

This decision solely depends on Maha Guru who is training that Guru.

After the Guru is certified to be ready to conduct a workshop by the Maha Guru, that Guru under training needs to organize 5 training sessions for that particular level in which he will be teaching everything completely by himself and initiating all the students from that batch by himself under Maha Guru's supervision.

Once a **Guru** completes the 4 levels of Vishitao Guru, he is certified as Vishitao Guru.

After a Vishitao Guru teachers at all these four levels for at least about a year and conducts at least 25 training sessions of each level of Vishitao, he is qualified to receive the Maha Guru's training.

The Maha Guru training goes in 2 phases, so it is a longer training. In the first phase, one learns how to make a Vishitao Guru, and in the second phase, one learns how to make a Vishitao Maha Guru.

In the first phase, the Maha Guru under training has organize & watch the training of at least 10 Vishitao Gurus just as he had his own training.

If the Maha Guru who is training a Maha Guru under training, feels, he may ask the Maha Guru under training to watch some more Guru trainings, till the Maha Guru is convinced that this Maha Guru under training has learned all the details.

This is because the Maha Guru is the highest Level of Vishitao. It is a level of immense responsibility.

Here, a Maha Guru can teach a healer to become a Vishitao Guru and can also teach a Guru to become Maha Guru of Vishitao.

Once a Maha Guru certifies that a Guru is ready to train another Guru under his supervision,

Then he must train at least two Vishitao Guru's under training, under the supervision of his Vishitao Maha Guru trainer.

After this, he has to organize & watch the training of at least 2 Vishitao Maha Gurus just as he had his own training.

Here, he must assist his Maha Guru in process of training of a Maha Guru.

Here, Maha Guru gives some additional tips to the Maha Guru under training.

These inputs are much deeper than the first phase of the Maha Guru training.

Once a Maha Guru certifies that a Guru is ready to train another Maha Guru under his supervision, Then he must train at least two Vishitao Guru's under the supervision of his Vishitao Maha Guru trainer.

During this time the Maha Guru trainer will train the Maha Guru under training for other things necessary in training.

This means out of the 9 stages of VISHITAO, the first four are the stages for a Vishitao Healer.

Only those who wish to take up teaching Vishitao as a profession may undergo training of next five levels.

BASIC LEVEL

1. Basic
2. Rules
3. Principles
4. Beginning of Vishitao Training
5. Vishitao
6. Kemizap
7. Practice needed by basic Vishitao healer

CHAPTER VI

Basic Vishitao

Vishitao method is a perfect combination of mind, body, plasma field balancing & harmonizing.

This is the reason why rules and principles of Vishitao work on the attitudes, thoughts, subconscious conditioning and innermost energy blocks and lets a healer create & manifest accurate and positive events to produce harmony.

Vishitao is useful in healing physical, mental, emotional, relationship, career and financial issues and in manifesting various events of our choice.

It can also be used to produce positive events in society around us. By this, each healer can do a lot of silent social service and spread positivity around in the world.

The best part of Vishitao is that here a healer does not have to touch the patient in any way whatsoever. So, at times, when we need to heal someone without his knowledge, we can very easily do so by using these Vishitao techniques.

In Indian and many conservative societies throughout the globe, touching by a stranger is not appreciated, so, this method is likely to be accepted by such societies very well.

Rules, Principles are tools of attitude work in the basic level of Vishitao.

CHAPTER VII

Rules of Vishitao:

When we practice Vishitao, we are expected to follow some rules in life.

These rules are not only helpful in effective healing, but are also helpful in leading a successful life.

These rules help us have right attitude, clarity of thinking to get everything that we deserve and we want in life.

These rules are very simple to remember and live. They are:

1. Keep away from EGO.
2. Keep away from struggle.
3. Keep away from complicating mind.
4. Keep away from force.
5. Keep away from distrust.

Let us see these rules in details:

Keep away EGO.

Since Vishitao represents mindless mind of universe, while using Vishitao, we MUST keep away our ego.

Keep away from struggle.

Never struggle while using Vishitao. The energy field will not work if we struggle.

Keep away from complicating mind.

Have clear vision of things or intentions. Don't complicate the vision.

Keep away from force.

If the energy field is not going to a certain event, know that what we have visualized needs amendment.

Keep away from distrust.

When we are not clear as to what has to be created in any particular situation to set it right, do not disbelieve your thinking or anything else. Just wish the natural harmony for the situation or ask for divine intervention in that area.

CHAPTER VIII

Principles of Vishitao:

To use Vishitao, follow the following principles:

1. I trust the natural harmony.
2. I will find out benefit in everything.
3. I will be humble when helping others.
4. I will be thankful to whatever I get.
5. I will be grounded and calm every time.
6. I will be a witness at all the times.
7. I will be positive in my attitude.
8. I will trust myself in whatever i do.
9. I trust in the goodness behind every evil.
10. I know that every event has two sides.

Let us see these principles in details:

1. I trust the natural harmony.

Nature has its own harmony that it keeps establishing every moment.

This harmony never lets any disharmony or wrong stay for long. Know this harmony, trust it, and know that even if we do nothing, things are still going to be normal in some time if left alone.

So we must never try to struggle for harmony and try to restore harmony beyond limit.

If need be, we can even trust the nature and stay away.

2. I look for benefit in everything.

Know that every experience always comes to us for a purpose. This purpose is beneficial for us.

It also stays with us till we take the whole benefit in that experience. So, instead of struggling or trying to get away from any experience, find out the benefit in that event for us and take it.

Remember, no one can ever progress without taking benefit out of every experience of life. It is this attitude of finding benefit that enriches us.

Every successful person has got success, due to this positive attitude.

3. I will be humble while helping all.

When we help others, if we feel that we are doing something great and we are favouring others by doing that thing, we develop Ego.

This ego is harmful for our being. So, we must stay humble and thankful when we are helping others.

We must remember that if they would not give an opportunity to help, we would never have got the pleasure of extending support.

So we must be grateful to them for letting us help them.

4. I will thank for whatever i get.

As we have already seen that everything that comes to us has a benefit for us, and everything or everyone who gives some benefit to us must be thanked.

So we must be thankful to everything and every experience that we get form others or from nature.

Remember, we can get the maximum benefit of anything only when we thank genuinely.

Also, thanking is better than forgiving as in forgiving, we have a thought that we are harmed and that thought prevents the benefit from coming to us, but when we thank, there is no prick of harm, so benefit comes freely.

5. I will be always grounded & calm.

If we find a problem in any situation, we generally get upset, disturbed or confused about the way out.

At such times, we must know that the situation also has a solution of that problem in it.

When we look at a situation more clearly, we can find out that solution. For this, a clam attitude is needed. So a healer must learn to stay grounded and calm.

6. I will be a witness at all the times.

When we are witnessing any event, we do not get involved in it and then we can see it from all possible angles.

On the other hand, when we are in any situation, we are able to see limited dimensions of that event as we are stuck with some angles of that situation.

So, in order to be able to have clear preview of any event or experience, we must be witness.

7. I will be positive in my attitude.

All people always teach us to have a positive attitude, but they rarely define it clearly.

Positive attitude is the one where we see all possible good things along with the bad things.

That means with a positive attitude, we see the advantage in an event and know that the disadvantages in it is the cost we are paying to get the advantages.

When we have a positive attitude, we look for the good points in every person's behaviour and also we look for good things in every event that we encounter.

This reduces anxiety and helps us extract maximum advantage out of any situation.

Such attitude always leads to success.

8. I will trust myself in all my acts.

When we trust ourselves, even others can trust us. When others trust us, they know our value, they respect us. When others respect us, we can get whatever we deserve.

When we get whatever we deserve, we get real happiness. So, it is evident that when we want to get everything that we deserve, we must begin with self trust.

9. I trust in good behind every evil.

At times events that come to us appear only bad or evil. It is hard to find any benefit in them.

Events like natural calamities or bad accidents are from such category.

Yet, we must know that even such events have some purpose and so, even such events have some value of goodness in them.

On recognising this fact we must look for goodness even in these events as we all know that after these events have happened, it is impossible to reverse their effects.

But the impact of these calamities can be mitigated with this attitude.

10. I know, each event has two sides.

We must know that every event has two sides. One is positive and other is negative.

This means, one side gives us some benefit whereas other causes some harm to us.

Yet, we generally see only one side of any event and label it as good or bad.

This attitude makes us rigid and then we become pessimistic with life.

This situation prevents us to move forward in life and we feel stuck and stagnated.

But when we recognise the presence of other side to every event, we are open to recognise it, accept it and benefit by the presence of this other side. Then we can move ahead and progress in life.

Know these principles, follow them in real life and make them an integral part of life.

When these principles become a part of our being, our life will transform and so will our spiritual self.

Then we will really be able to do a great service to our planet Mother Earth!

CHAPTER IX

Beginning of Vishitao Training:

The training of Basic VISHITAO healing methods begins with the method of learning how to create energy field. For creating an energy field, sit with your spine straight.

1. Keep hands in receiving position over thighs.
2. Close your eyes
3. Put your tongue tip touching upper pallet.
4. Take deep breath,
5. Hold it as long as you can and slowly release.
6. Do this for 11 times.
7. Then place your palms facing each other
8. Keep around 6 inches distance between them.
9. With your palms in this position
10. Close your eyes
11. Put our tongue tip touching upper pallet centre.
12. Take deep breath,
13. Hold it as long as you can and slowly release.
14. Do this for 21 times.

Now feel the energy ball between our palms.

We are supposed to heal or create events in VISHITAO with the help of this is the energy field.

Once we learn to create energy field we must learn to visualize events that we wish to create.

For this, first decide whom we wish to heal or which event we wish to create.

Then try to note the details of the person/event as much as we can.

Remember, more details we visualize faster the event we wish to create, comes to material reality & gets manifested.

When we get good practice of visualizing the event clearly, we must go to the next level where we create energy field.

Visualize the event of our choice and visualize the energy ball we have created around the event we wish to create.

When we can do this effectively we are ready to heal with the help of the Vishitao delineations.

Before actually learning to heal with the delineations now we must first learn the delineations.

In basic level of Vishitao we have two delineations. Vishitao & Kemizap

CHAPTER X

1. Vishitao-wish:

This delineation energises our energy field.

While drawing this, we first draw a golden circle.

Then we draw a golden star inside that circle.

All the points of our star touch the circle.

Then we draw a purple diamond inside the pentagon in the center of this star.

Vishitao

We simply visualize this delination and draw it mentally on the energy field we create every time while healing with Vishitao.

The circle protects the energy field we have created & are sending from being disintegrated & decomposed.

The star collects 5 elements and brings them to our intention.

The diamond focuses divine light over our intention.

So we draw this to empower our wish before we insert our wish in the energy field we have created.

Once we insert our wish in the energy field, we again draw Vishitao to strengthen it.

CHAPTER XI

2. Kemizap-bridge:

Kemizap is a delineation that is drawn with a large number of different colours.

We first draw a purple 7.

Then we draw another purple 7, but sleeping with the upper straight line of 7 pointing downwards on our right side.

Then, below it, we draw inverted curved "V" in indigo colour.

Then we draw a red sleeping 7 with the upper straight line of 7 pointing downwards on our right side.

Then we draw three brown 7s below this red sleeping 7.

Then we draw a green Theta like image where the line inside circle begins from center and touches only the right side of circle.

Then we again draw two yellow sleeping 7s under each other.

This whole drawing makes the delination of Kemizap.

Kemizap

Kemizap has the power to create a bridge or link between our mind and the event that we wish to manifest into reality, with the help of the universal mind.

It can connect we to the event we wish to create so that with the help of further delineations we can bring it to material reality.

When we are working with this system, and when we are visualizing the events we wish to create, we create these events mentally.

After we have created these events mentally, we must remember that these events are present somewhere in the universe in some suitable form.

We need to search for them in the universe and manifest them in material reality at the time and place as we want them to happen.

Kemizap helps we do this effectively.

When we are using the Basic VISHITAO method we are using just Vishitao and Kemizap.

These two delineations help we energise the energy field we create.

When we heal at basic level, we create energy field visualize the event put energy field still in our hands around the visualized event image & Kemizap over the field.

When we have done all this just release the energy field and let it go into the existence to manifest the event.

We may do it daily till event manifest.

CHAPTER XII

Practice needed by basic Vishitao healer

So, as a Basic Vishitao Healer, we must make the rules and principles a part of our life and attitudes.

One must follow both these things in their daily activities.

We must choose the events to create with responsibility, visualize them well.

Then work to create them till they come to reality.

We must not make any unrealistic and tall claims when we are working to create any event or to heal anyone.

At the same time, we must not have any doubt or negative attitude while working.

This means, a Basic vishitao healer must work to create energy ball almost every day at least for two or three events or healings.

As a healer is doing all this, he must also check the results and maintain a track of results he achieved in healing and manifesting events.

All this is needed as unless the foundation is not strong, there is no sense in starting the further construction of knowledge and wisdom.

Also, Vishitao is the energy work of very high responsibility. So, unless one is not fully ready with the basic level, there is no sense in going for the further levels.

As soon as we are confident enough to create an energy field and to put basic delineations on it and send it, we can go to the further level of Vishitao.

MATERIAL LEVEL

1. Material level
2. Active Gratitude
3. Active Grounding
4. Reymzen
5. Mertiori
6. Awem
7. O Tu Se
8. Hon Sui
9. Ri Me Ga
10. Polora
11. Swe
12. Grim
13. Sil
14. Metra
15. Kshed
16. Practice needed by a material level healer

CHAPTER XIII

Material level Vishitao:

Vishitao Healer has already learned the attitude necessary to heal effectively in the basic level.

Here, he has to practice and revise it. A Material level healer must understand that we have four elements around us that influence us. This is because they all are on earth and are directly connected to us.

These are, earth, water fire and air. Space is the fifth element but that is on our earth as well as all over the universe. So, we do not count space here.

These components are our own self, controllable circumstances, uncontrollable circumstances and external environment. While dealing with these components, we try to satisfy them, deal with their needs and deal with the emergencies created in and around them.

While doing so, we use various people and resources around and keep an account of our benefits and losses. As we do this, we learn many things. We also teach many things to people around us.

We can plan our future activities towards goals and while doing so, we negotiate with circumstances. We enrol others into our plans and programs by way of convincing them. We handle the rule structures that our society gives.

In our daily activities, we identify our needs. We organise resources. We monitor speed of performance and task completion. We plan future needs, predict and handle emergencies. This organizes directs and plans events.

While dealing with situations, we identify aspects, gather information and relate them with situations.

In our daily activities, we follow some basic management principles, viz,

1. Target setting,
2. Problem solving
3. Being a Leader
4. Building support
5. Dealing with emergencies

We need to imbibe the 5 types of skills to be a perfect human being. These skills are:

1. Intellectual
2. Technical
3. Ethical
4. Interactive
5. Emotional

We must organise desires in systematic way to let them become material reality. For it, we follow some steps:

1. Dreams / visions
2. Barriers in their achievement
3. Ways to avoid barriers
4. Ways to handle barriers
5. Steps to be taken to bypass barriers
6. Benefits in hiding behind barriers
7. Benefits in handling barriers
8. Visualising details of dream
9. Benefit of detailed visualization
10. Energising positive thoughts.

To be able to manage situation perfectly, one has to work on his mind and attitudes by doing some basic mind work exercise. He can do this exercise daily.

When one follows basic ways of positive thinking, one can use the healing and event manifesting delineations very effectively.

This level helps we manifest the physical events and produce the healing.

What we need to do is draw the delineations over the energy field just as basic level after the first two basic delineations.

This level has many delineations. We need not use all at one time.

We have to choose the delineations and their combinations to produce the specific event or healing we wish to create and fulfill our material desires.

There are contradictory delineations like healing and cooling, increasing and decreasing.

Do not use them together or the effect will be nullified. Choose the delineations from this list properly.

Let us see this exercise:

CHAPTER XIV

Active Gratitude:

Active Gratitude

- Sit in a comfortable position. Close your eyes.
- Think of all who helped you.
- Think of the benefit you got out of the help.
- Thank them.
- Think of all those who harmed you.
- Find the benefit you got through that harm.
- Thank them.
- Think of those whom you helped.
- Find the benefit you got out of that help.
- Thank them.
- Think of those whom you harmed.
- Mentally ask forgiveness for harm you did.
- Think of benefits you both got from the harm.
- Thank them for tolerating you.
- Think of natural resources that contributed.
- Thank them.
- Feel the gratitude everywhere.
- Find yourself thankful to all creation of god.
- Slowly open your eyes & start your routine.

CHAPTER XV

Active Grounding:

Active Grounding:

- Sit in a comfortable position.
- Close your eyes.
- Concentrate on your breathing.
- Be aware of the energies around.
- Be aware of your thoughts.
- Find the thoughts that make you comfortable.
- Find the thoughts that make you restless.
- Know that this is due to non-grounding.
- Let the divine love shower on you.
- Let these energies enter through top of head.
- Let these energies fill your body.
- Feel the comfort with these energies.
- Let the disturbing thought get energy roots.
- Let these roots go into the ground.
- Request the roots to reach problem solution.
- Feel the relief from the upsets.
- Now let the divine love create total rooting.
- Have perfectly grounded practical attitude.
- Slowly open your eyes and start the routine

CHAPTER XVI

1. Reymzen – Healing:

This delineation is useful in producing effective healing.

The first step towards drawing this is the golden star.

Below this star, we draw three verticle lines of same height, such that extreme left is golden green, middle is red and extreme right is indigo blue.

Below this is the curved inverted v of baby pink colour.

Then we draw a dark pink small line inside this inverted curved V.

Below this, we draw a circle that is half black & half white, such that the left side of it is black and right side is white.

Below this, we have a dark pink angular inverted U with a small horizontal line in its center.

Below it, we have a light blue curved M like figure.

Below it, we have a dark pink curved E like figure.

Below it, there is yellow sleeping T, where the T making horizontal line, that is now verticle, is surrounded by a dark pink half circle, forming a -D like figure.

Below it is a dark purple spiralgoing clockwise from inside towards out.

At the end, we draw a golden sleeping 7 below this purple spiral.

This is how we draw the complete delination of Reymzen.

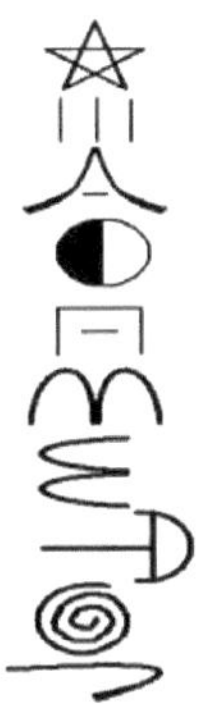

Reymzen

This healing is produced with the help of two main things.

The Panchatanmatras, i.e. the five subtle elements, viz, Earth, Water, Fire, Air & Space are represented by the Golden Star.

The Triguna beejas, i.e. three subtle gunas or qualities, viz. Sattva = positivity, Rajas = Power, Tamas = Destroying ability, (represented by Generator organizer and destroyer) present in universe & controlled by universal mind, are represented by three lines, green orange & indigo below the star.

We collect them with love and send the energies down to our production. This is indicated by two pink curved lines spread like a root & a pink line between, indicating seed of healing energy.

We bring them down through the black & white circle, to create a perfect harmony of positive and negative that leads to the Shunya state.

Then we draw three lines as the upper three lines of a square in pink and draw a pink line in the centre of this. This line structure indicates balance of downloaded energies.

This means that due to our energy work done till now, we have brought down energies, but they may be having some inherent imbalance, which is corrected and a perfect harmony is established.

Then we ground it. This grounding is indicated by the blue 'm' like sign.

Also in this process, we bring the future harmony into the present. This is indicated by the pink 'E' like sign.

Then we release the factors that disturb this harmony from the ailing person. This is indicated by the yellow sleeping 'T' and pink 'D' curve.

When all this is done, we accelerate the process. This is done by the purple clockwise spirals moving outward from the centre.

Then we ground the healing. This is represented by the yellow line with tilted tip.

How to use Reymzen:

While using this delineation, visualize the total body of the patient, draw Vishitao & Kemizap on the energy field with the patient in it.

Then draw Reymzen. Now send the energy field to the patient. Desire the total healing of the patient.

(For better results, cover the patient with Polora at the end of the healing session.)

CHAPTER XVII

2. Metiori – Desire:

This delineation is drawn in orange colour.
Here we draw a tilted orange W.
Then we pull the last line downward.
Then we take it upward to connect with begining point.
This goes through all three lines forming N like figure.
It connects with the begining point of the first W.
The line going up joins the beginning point of Metiori.
This is how we draw the delination Metiori.
It is fully orange in colour.

Metiori

In the process of drawing this delination, the direction of lines going downwards, again coming up and going down and coming up and going down indicate out attitude in handling the obstacles in creation of event.

This has the power to strengthen desire that we have,

It can energize the event we visualize, manifests with maximum force and comes to reality easily.

In this process, it reduces our feeling of struggle and the obstacles that we unknowingly create due to this struggle.

Many times, people struggl to bring their desire into reality, but that struggle in fact reduces the force of their manifestation further.

In such situations, we find ourselves in a vicious circle.

Metiori helps we come out of this vicious circle.

To use this, visualize our desire coming true and draw this on the energy field.

CHAPTER XVIII

3. Awem – Unity

Awem enables to produce unity in two persons or groups that cannot be together.

While drawing awem, we first draw a 'z' and inverted 'z' intersecting each other in dark pink.

Then we fill the two rectangles created by this intersection by baby pink.

We draw a shape like 'S' in gold colour at both opposite intersecting crosses.

We draw sleeping '3' and its vertically turned version on both points of intersection of the two rectangles.

This indicates establishing and developing of the broken relation to form unity

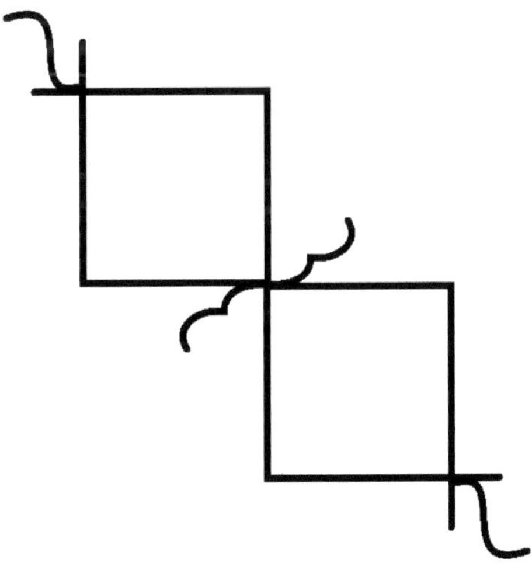

Awem

Many people or groups have severe differences.

They end up, in depleting their energies constantly fighting with each other.

Even then we try to motivate them to unite, we fail.

At such times, just use this delineation on visualizing them together in the energy field.

Draw it after the basic delineations and send the energy field to the two together.

CHAPTER XIX

4. O Tu Se – Relationship

This delineation is good to heal general relationships of a person, as well as to heal and strengthen the relationships of people.

To draw this, we use two intersecting circles, drawn in yellow.

We fill the separate sections of these circles in pink.

The intersecting area is white, but it has a dark pink diamond in it.

This diamond creates and nurtures the relationship between two individuals or groups, who are represented by the two golden circles.

Of the relationship between two needs healthy strengthening, this delineation works wonderfully.

It creates a harmonious relationship between tow people.

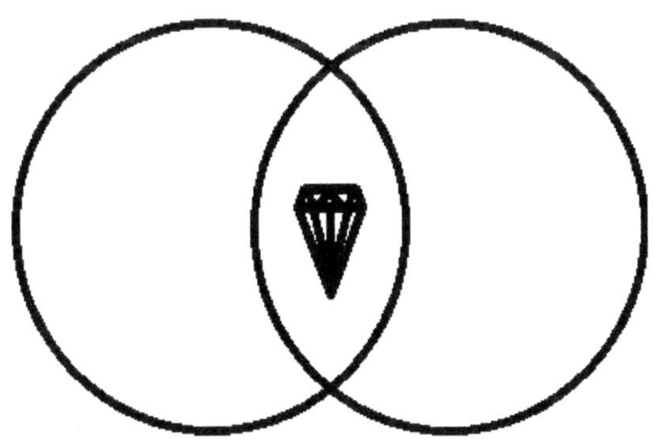

O Tu Se

O tu se is useful in creating healthy relationship.

Such relationship can be created between two people or two groups, or one person and one group and any such combination.

To use this, we just have to visualize the two persons or groups or one person and one group; between whom we wish to create a good relation, in the energy field we have created,

Then we must draw the first mendatory delinations.

Then we put the delineation O Tu Se on the energy field.

We must clearly visualize those whose relation we must strengthen quite clearly.

Then, while visualizing the images clearly, we must send the energy ball to the existence.

CHAPTER XX

5. Hon Sui - Rooting:

This delineation helps to ground the event we have visualized and speed up the process of manifestation.

While drawing this delineation the two purple double curves indicate the showering divine blessings.

The three lines with curved tip show acceptance of the blessings.

Yellow downward curve indicate emotional receptivity to blessings.

Brown double curve & the line in between represent grounding of blessing within our system.

Yellow twin 'T', i.e. 'TT' delineates the perfect grounding of the blessings on emotional level.

The inverted orange 'U', i.e. '| |' indicate the courage being developed due to blessings.

The dark green bottom line delineates fertilised grounding of the received energies.

The two light green sprouts emerging out of the green line indicate the beginning of prosperity.

All this make this a perfect grounding delineation where we can create total inner harmony with the goodluck received from the universe and with the total acceptance of all goodness around.

Each colour as well as shape here has specific picture language significance.

Hon Sui

This is a delination of Grounding.

We use it to created grounded practical attitude in people around.

If we wish that a person develops a realistic attitude visualize him in the energy field we create and draw this delineation over the energy field.

Then we must send the energy field to the existence which will create necessary changes in that person.

When we wish to manifest an event, we have to ground the event visualized.

We must draw it over the event after using all other delineations before releasing the field.

CHAPTER XXI

6. Ri Me Ga - Abundance:

Ri Me Ga is a delineation that attracts prosperity, abundance & affluence to the seeker.

We begin drawing Ri Me Ga with two purple inverted V curves one below the other.

Two purple twin curves represent divine luck shower.

Inside both these inverted Vs, we draw small blue lines.

Blue lines inside curves represent physical acceptance of good luck.

Below it, we draw a dark pink curved m.

Pink 'm' like shows affectionate loving assimilation of affluent good luck.

Then we draw a half circle with open ends down.

This has golden yellow colour on outer surface.

The inner surface is golden green.

The yellow curve is emotional acceptance of affluence.

Inner green curve within is the inner healing resulting in removal of scarcity feeling.

Below this, we draw a brown straight line ouching both open ends of the above half circle.

The brown sleeping line represents ground.

Below this, we draw an orange verticle line forming a T with brown horizontal & orange verticle line.

and the orange standing line below, that forms a 'T' shape, indicates rooting of abundance energies.

At the end, we draw a red cross, not like +, but like the cristian cross; under this T.

The Red Cross below is solid anchor inside ground that keeps abundance and prosperity.

This is how we draw Ri Me Ga.

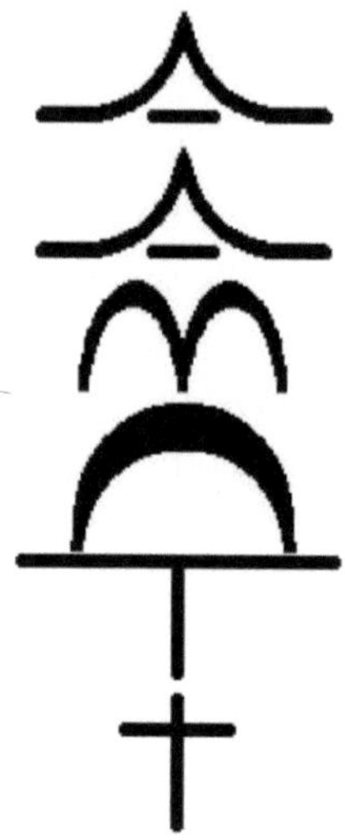

Ri Me Ga

This is a pictorial representation of the process of developing abundance & affluence in our life.

This delineation helps to generate affluence of life with abundance in all means of life.

It helps us receive all things from existence.

It takes away fear and scarcity from all areas of our life.

Remember, many times, people have all the wealth, but they still do not have the affluent quality of life.

This is because, though they have money, they still don't have abundance within.

To overcome scarcity and have abundance, we draw Ri Me Ga over energy field after removing thoughts of scarcity.

This delineation will manifest abundance.

CHAPTER XXII

7. Polora - Protection:

Whenever we create any event mentally to manifest it on the material plane, we need togive it a strong protection.

Polora is a delination for the same.

While drawing polora, we start from innermost point.

This is a green coloured diamond.

Around it, we draw a golden star.

We cover this star by drawing an indigo circle around it.

Beyond indigo circle, we draw a electric violet circle.

Beyond electric violet circle, we draw a golden circle.

This is how we draw Polora.

Polora

This time, we visualize the person or event to be protected, inside the green diamon in the center of it.

This delineation has capacity to give total protection to a person or event visualized in energy field.

With the protection, the events or persons can be kept away from negative and hostile thoughts and energies.

Once Polora is drawn, thoughts or energies cannot disturb the harmony that the other delineations establish in the even or person.

Since this is a protection delineation, it has to be drawn, at the time of releasing the energy field after all other delineations are drawn.

CHAPTER XXIII

8. Swe - motion:

Swe is a delination that is quite easy to draw.

It is also quite meningful.

It has six golden spikes.

They are made of three straight lines.

These are lines intersecting each other in the centre.

Then we draw red circles at the end point of each line that forms the end of each of the six spikes.

When we draw swe over the energy field, we also visualize the spikes moving clockwise taking the energy field ahead towards our destination with great speed.

This is how we draw Swe.

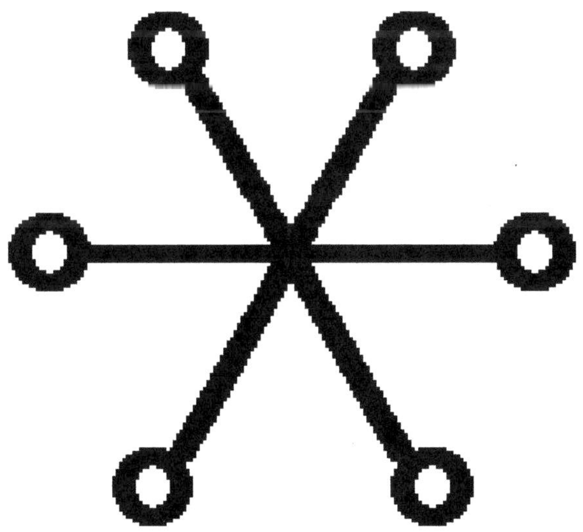

Swe

This is delineation of motion when we wish to set something in motion, we can use this delineation.

Also when we wish to accelerate the process of healing, we use this delineation to increase the acceleration.

To set some event in motion, use this on the energy field after we draw other delineations to create them.

Also, to start the process of healing or creating the event faster, we use this while releasing the energy field with event in it.

This means, most of the times, after energy field is created, other relatd delinations are drawn over the event seen in the energy field, we draw swe at the end.

CHAPTER XXIV

9. Grim- heat:

Grim is fire or heat prducng delineation.

It stands for physical manifestation of fire.

It is used to generate heat or even fire in physical form.

The colour of this is red & brown.

The fire flame like curves can be 10 or more as per need of intensity of heat to be generated.

The bottom line indicates grounding of this heat, so, it is brown in colour.

So it represents red fire colur for creating heat or fire with brown colour or ground indicating that this fire created is well grounded.

Grim

This delineation represents flame of fire when we wish to increase heat in some area of the body or in some place put this delineation over the energy field and release if.

Whenever the atmosphere is too cold, we can use this on the energy ball.

Then we may place the energy ball containing it around us.

This will make us feel warm.

If the body of a person is getting cold due to weakness, we can place the energy ball containing this delineation around that person.

It will generate the necessary amount of heat in the necessary area or part of body.

This may save that person.

This means, if we wish to produce heat in physical form anywhere, Grim is the solution.

Generally one must use this delineation in combination with other appropriate delineations.

But for producing atmospheric we can use just this delineation over the energy field that we send to atmosphere.

CHAPTER XXV

10. Sil - cooling:

Unlike other well-known healing modalities, Vishitao is the only one that has power to work even on pysical things like temperature.

Grim that we saw just now is a heating delination while Sil is a cooling delineation.

The two lines of five blue waves represent the cold energy from universe.

Dark blue bottom line represents absorption & assimilation of that cold energy.

This absorption is done to produce physical cooling.

This is a material level delineation.

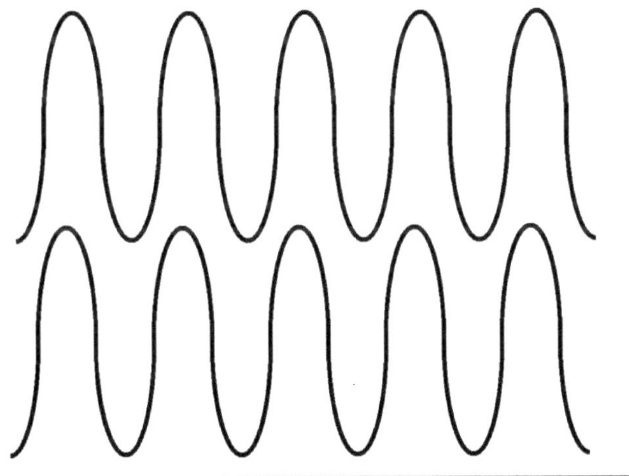

Sil

This delineation represents water with waves.

So, an energy ball with sil produces physical cooling.

Just as water is cooling and produces necessary amount of cooling, even Sil is meant for producing necessary amount of cooling in the events or atmosphere or body.

When the ailment is caused due to excess of heat in the body this delineation proves to be useful in healing along with other delineations for healing.

At times, when the weather is too hot, and there is no way to handle the heat.

At such times, we can put this delineation on the area in the energy field and send.

CHAPTER XXVI

Grim-Sil Group

Grim an sil are the two unique symbols that are not found in any other healing modality.

The globe knows about hundreds of healing modalities.

Some get popular, some take time to get known.

Some methods like local medicines of each place, still stay in dark after hundreds of years of serving humanity.

These two symbols make Vishitao unique.

In fact, all known healing modalities wok at the mind level and let the mind level affect the material level.

But the Grim-sil group of symbols is a unique combo that actually works on material level without mind intervention by the one who is receiving the healing.

The healer directly commands the atmosphere around to increase or decrease the temperature with the help of these symbols.

Some Vishitao students have even generated warm bathing water in the winter after experiencing a breakdown of gayser.

It shows the immense power of these delinations.

We all know about Yogis who live almost without clothing in the freezing temperature of himalayan ranges without getting affectedbadversely by the coldness of the snow around. It is certainly the same power of grim and sil that works in such situations.

Naturally, Those who learn vishitao and also wish to serve humanity and society in general, can certainly send a warm protection shield to all our soldiers on the border who are working in all odd situations just to protect us!

Whenever I announce some discounted workshops of vishitao, I ask the seekersto pay the amount they have saved, not by cash, but by kind by serving the sildiers of their own nation as and when they can see the need.

This is how, during vishitao training, we encourage every healer to fulfill his or her own social responsibility.

We must use both Grim and Sil with responsibility.

Producing temperature changes in atmosphere, body, object, machine etc is needed urgently many times.

At such times, we do not have resources to do so in any normal way.

At such situations, Sil and Grim work wonders.

This means, at times, both Grim and Sil can work as life savers for individuals, groups of people or nature or machines or even factories etc.

There are many techniques of energy work taught, but these two are totally unique and seen ONLY & ONLY in Vishitao.

CHAPTER XXVII

11. Metra - creation:

Metra is a delineation of any creation manifested.

This is drawn in golden and electric violet colours.

This delination begins with a golden star in centre.

This is the point where creation of our desired event germinates.

The desired event that is germinated here inside the golden star.

Then it grows under the protection of this golden star.

Once it is ready, its moves towards materialization.

Then we see the next part of the delination happening in the form of purple clockwise spirals.

This is representation of the journey of the created event towards materialization.

This journey is indicated by the purple clockwise spirals starting at the top of the star, growing outwards.

The symbolic expression of this delination is that the imagined event germi8nates and grows inside the star in the centre an then, follows the electric violate clockwise spiral path of the divine will in order to manifest itself in actual reality.

Here, the number of spirals we use while drawing this delination, depend on the need or speed we want in manifesting of that event in material reality.

When we want a speedy manifestation of the event, we draw many spirals and if we are ok to give a reasonable time for th manifestation, we may draw less spirals.

Yet minimum number of spirals expected is at least 3.

Metra

To create something we can use Metra effectively.

We use it on events that we feel may not manifest easily.

Since it is a delineation of creation, it should be used in creating things and events etc.

This means, it need not be used when we are modifying or healing anything.

It will work only in creating new things.

To use this, visualize the event we visualize the area where we want if to manifest and then put the vision in the energy field, draw this after the basic delineations and release the field.

CHAPTER XXVIII

12. Kshed - breaking:

Kshed is breaking manifested.

The delineation has a red arrow moving upward to right. This represents breaking future barriers.

The green curve around this arrow is the positive energy support given to arrow to break negatives.

At times we may find that there are some sticky energy that is not leaving a person or event.

They may keep sticking there and obstruct the healing and harmony.

These energies need forceful breaking. Kshed does this. It effectively breaks energies causing imbalance with this.

Kshed

Remember Kshed works only on constructive breaking. To use Kshed visualize the area with sticky energies and having it in every field, draw Kshed and send.

CHAPTER XXIX

Practice needed by Material level Practitioners:

The Material level uses the regular power energy that we receive with the attunement while learning this healing method. Later delineations can pull more energy from universe.

These are the delineations of the physical level of healing. With these one can heal quite effectively the physical events and ailments.

We need to choose the right combination of delineations as per the need. Generally of we are doing regular meditations, we may get the right combination as an intuition. Still as a hint I am giving some tips:

- Begin with Vishitao and Kemizap.
- For healing purpose, use Reymzen with the required other delineations and Polora.
- For getting abundance, use Hon Sui and Ri Mega.
- For event creation, use Metra and Swe.
- For healing relations, use Reymzen with O tu se or Awem and then use Hon Sui.
- For reducing heat in atmosphere around, use sil
- For reducing coldness around, use Grim
- For removing wrong things around, first protect good people with polora and then by creating next energy field, send Kshed and swe on wrong things.
- To remove bad habits in people around, visualize the bad thought in them and draw kshed.

- We may think of many more delineation combinations like this.
- Vishitao seekers at material level may certainly visualize many more combinations
- They can also share and discuss these new combos with other vishitao seekers.
- Also, after or while learning the VISHITAO at this level,
- When you think of or see some new combinations, please feel free to share them with us by sending a whatsapp message on 9820044254 or 9870044254.
- This will help us to see ti it that those things can be incorporated in our next edition of this book.

Later on after doing the next two levels, it is possible to use these delineations in combination with the delineations of those levels that would make the work more powerful.

MENTAL LEVEL:

1. Mental level
2. Mind Body Relation
3. Emotions Connected with body
4. Negative Attitudes, Causes & Sources
5. Impact of negative attitudes
6. Effects of negative thinking
7. Negative attitude and life
8. Negative personality types
9. Changing negative attitudes into positive
10. Mindork for Active empowerment
11. Megi
12. Som
13. Stroc
14. Megrow
15. Mellow
16. Chi hon swe
17. Practice needed by Mental level healer

CHAPTER XXX

Mental Level Vishitao:

This level helps us get additional support from divine minds of masters in astral form.

In this level, a healer learns basic mind-body relationship. He learns that an appropriate attitude is absolutely necessary to produce desired events.

There is a general conception of people that positive attitude is necessary to be happy in life, but no one defines this positive attitude.

Many people say that having hope that good things will happen, and not talking of things that we do not want to happen is positive attitude.

But is it really so? We need to think deeply.

Many times, we want something to happen. But at the same time, we have fear and doubt whether our wish will come true or not.

Then we forcefully keep our thought of fear away. At least, we do not express that fear.

Is it positive attitude? No. Because, at such times, without our knowledge, our fear sends negative energy to our wish and even if our wish is simple, we block the fulfilment of that wish unknowingly by our fear and doubt.

Later, when our wish does not come true, we may blame some energies or persons for blocking and preventing the fulfilment of our wish. We even go to an extent that we feel some one has done a psychic attack on us, so this happened. But we never realize that that our own thoughts are the real blocks between our wishes and their fulfilment.

Here in the mental level of Vishitao, a healer understands the type of attitudes and thoughts that produce negative results, though they are not apparently considered as negative thoughts.

At times, they are called thoughts of concern or care expressed by people in every society.

Negative thoughts drain us of energy and keep us from being in the present moment.

The more we give in to our negative thoughts, the stronger they become.

They act like a small ball rolling along the ground; as it rolls, it becomes bigger and faster.

Exactly like the small rolling ball growing big, one small negative thought has a potential to turn into a huge, speeding ball of ugliness.

On the other hand, a small positive thought that enhances our self trust, has power to blossom into a beautiful outcome of our desired event.

When one nurtures negative thinking, a small thought turns into very bad & negative experience.

When we start having negative thoughts, it's hard to stop them.

It's much easier said than done to shift our focus to positive thoughts.

But shifting to positive thoughts is the only way, to avoid the tragedies we are likely to invite with our thoughts; especially if we want to avoid going down a path that is painful and unnecessary.

We must know why we must change our thinking and take steps to stop thinking negatively.

We can live a much richer, more enjoyable, more successful life without the consequences of negative thinking, if we know this fact.

The more our mind understands this, the more our mind is energized and motivated to help us stop thinking negatively.

In this way, this awareness helps us to get rid of negative thinking faster and easier.

To handle negative thoughts we must know the causes of negative attitude.

Attitude is the way of being of one's mind. It is a way in which we look at any situation. It marks a set of pre existing ideas in our mind about a person, event or situation.

Yet, attitude is not to be mistaken for prejudice; because prejudice is only negative, attitude may be negative or positive.

Negative and positive are purely subjective terms. They apply to both thoughts and actions.

Negative is something that blocks directly or indirectly, implicitly or explicitly, verbally or by act.

Positive is something that opens all the gates directly or indirectly, implicitly or explicitly, verbally or non-verbally; by actions.

CHAPTER XXXI

Mind body relation:

We all know that a healthy mind stays in a healthy body and vice versa. If mind loses health, the body becomes unhealthy in some time.

Similarly, if body is unhealthy, mind becomes irritable. It is medically proved that 99% of the ailments originate in the mind. So, when we know the psychology of ailments, we can remove the root cause of it from the mind, both with Vishitao and counseling.

A good Vishitao healer must remember that he has to remove the root cause of problem. If a person is sick, it is because, he has invited the sickness subconsciously for some payoff.

We must make a patient aware of this without offending him and make his mind clear that he need not invite ailment for he is not going to get any benefit by that.

This means, we must talk to him and also provide him some counseling that can help him locate, accept and then release the thoughts and emotions that have made him sick.

When we do this successfully, Vishitao works faster and the ailment once healed, does not recur.

We know that even the most dreaded ailment like cancer recurs a few years, even after chemo therapy, when root cause from mind of patient is not removed.

Same thing happens in many ailments, and so, removing roots of the ailment from the mind is absolutely necessary.

For doing this, we must find out the problem that a patient is having, analyze it and then conclude the type of thought or emotion that is bugging him.

Generally, when one experiences a shock, it has impact on the body part that is connected with that type of shock.

But in such case, the part of the body does not get afected immediately; it gets affected after about six to eight months from the time of getting a shock.

So, when a patient approaches, on seeing the symptoms, a healer may refer to the table of emotions and body parts and ask the patient relevant questions.

From the answers we get, the healer may get to know how much he is accurate.

Then he can also start combining various Vishitao methods to heal the patient quickly and effectively.

CHAPTER XXXII

Emotions connected with body:

Here are the emotions connected with major areas of the body;

Nose: Related to heart, sense & smell and sexual Response self-recognition

Mouth: Survival issues, capacity to take in new ideas.

Fore Head: Intellectual expression

Neck: Intellectual thoughts and emotions come together stiffness in neck is due to withheld statements.

Face: Face expresses various masks of our personality face also shows how we face world.

Eyes: How we see the world Window of soul

Eye brows: Emotional expressions

3rd Eye: intuitive center.

Ears: Our capacity to hear

Jaw: Whenever there is a tension here indicates blockage of emotional and verbal communications. Fear of expression.

Arms and Hands: These are extensions of heart centre. Expresses love and emotion both giving and receiving creativity ability

Chest: Relationship issues.

Heart: Love and emotion.

Solar Plexus: Power issues Wisdom center.

Abdomen: Seat of emotion. Our deepest feelings stored.

Genitals: Related to root chakra Survival issues Fear of life and existence

Thigh: Personal strength Trust in once own ability

Knees: Fear of death, Fear of death of once own self or ego, Fear of change of Responsibility.

Feet: It shows how we are grounded, Connected with reaching our goals, Fear of completion.

Back: Where we store our unconscious emotions and tensions here.

Shoulders: Responsibilities area like Carrying weight of the world. Fear of responsibility.

Upper Back: Anger

Lower Back: Men, particularly, store their emotions.

Pelvis/Ovary: Seat of KUNDALINI energy, Root of basic survival needs.

Calf Muscles: Self control issues

Lower Leg: Fear of action and enabling movement towards goals.

Ankles: Creates balance

Let's see the negative attitudes in details, so that we can understand ways to handle them.

CHAPTER XXXIII

Negative attitudes; Causes and sources:

Everything has a cause and so even a negative thought has a cause. If we know the cause & handle it, we can to remove an unwanted effect. This is true with negative thoughts as well. So, we must know the causes of negative thoughts that limit us.

We must list them and then understand each cause well, so that we can handle these causes and do not let them hinder our life in future. We can also work on negative and limiting the thoughts of our near & dear by this knowledge.

Here are some major causes of negative attitude:

1. Limiting Beliefs
2. Negativc family/friends
3. Deliberate efforts of others
4. Inability to make choices
5. Negative environment
6. Unsatisfying circumstances in life

Limiting beliefs:

The cause of negative attitude is wrong belief about life or certain aspects of it. You see the life through your beliefs and if your beliefs are negative, you will see your life as unhappy or downright pointless. To change such attitude you need to change your beliefs.

Negative family and/or friends:

Our friends or family affect us. If we are in a family where family members are negative, such a family causes bad attitude. If we have friends who are negative, and try to control us, and always talk about things that make us feel bad, we develop a negative attitude. Yet, even in such situations, we can decide how to feel. We and only we can decide how to react to anything that happens to us.

Deliberate efforts of others:

At times, people take special efforts to make us upset and negative. This is simply because eithet they are negative themselves or because they enjoy seeing others suffer. So, whenever one provokes us to become negayive, we don't have to get upset when someone tries to get you upset. We can always choose to remain calm or even be happy. If we allow others to decide how we should feel, we let them have control over us. That's, not a wise decision since people usually mind their own well-being first. Also, majority of people take pleasure in seeing others suffer.

Inability to make choices:

If your family is negative, you can choose to keep at safe distance with it. If your friends are negative, you can refuse to be with them. This will be beneficial as then no one will give you negative beliefs and thus cause your negative attitude. Remember, you attract your friends and because of that you have the power to attract better ones.

Negative environment:

If you do not see any relation between your thoughts & environment that you find yourself in, you are sure to assume that you have no power to change it. So when you think you are powerless and your environment is negative that causes your negative attitude. To change your negative environment you need to change your thinking which will be described further on in this article.

Unsatisfying circumstances in life:

If you are complaining about how unhappy you are, it's because you have a negative attitude. It may be hard at first to understand and accept this but the quicker you do, the quicker you will be able to change your life for the better. Your complaining alone can keep you stuck in the circumstances that you find unsatisfying. So to change your life you should stop complaining and start working on improving your life.

CHAPTER XXXIV

Impact of negative attitudes

When a person is negative, his personality stinks.

He keeps spreading negative energies just by his presence.

This means, people with negtive attitude, not only create blocks and barriers in life of others, but they also have potent to turn positive people into negative.

Negative attitudes not only create bitterness, but also create problems in life of people who have negative attitude.

In short, negative attitudes have destructive potential can not only destroy others, but also destroy those who have, nurture and spread negative attitudes.

These attitudes have two types of impacts, immediate and long lasting.

The immediate impact is that whenever we encounter a negative person, we give up the idea of doing any constructive work with such a person.

Here, the negative person as well as society become a loser.

The long lasting impact of negative attitude is that it works like a slow poison in project on which the negative person is working along with others.

So, whenever we come across negative attitude, we must keep the people with such attitudes at a safe distance. This is because, some attitudes have a dangerous immediate negative impact on our lives.

IMMEDIATE NEGATIVE IMPACT:

Negative thinking has an immediate, destructive impact on our life, because the moment we have a negative thought, it's already:

- Hindering us from achieving something that we want
- Making us feel worse
- Adding negative value to our life in some way

This means that there are no benefits of negative thinking like the benefits that exist with positive thinking.

With this in mind, we know about how negative thinking adversely affects our life.

- **Hindering us from achieving something that we want:** Negative thoughts become obstacles and prevent us from achieving what we say we want to achieve.

- **Making us feel worse:** Negative thoughts make us feel extremely & disproportionately worse & worthless in any adverse situation.
- **Adding negative value to our life in some way:** Negative thought add negative value to life & make it miserable.

This means, the moment we entertain anyone passing negative comments towards any thing, unknowingly, we invite negativity in our life. So, if we wish that our life stays happy, we must see to it that we are away from direct or indirect connection with anything that smells negative.

CHAPTER XXXV

Effects of negative thinking

Negative thinking is knowingly or unknowingly done by people due to a few conscious or sub-conscious reasons.

Some think, speak or act negatively due to, Fear of future, anxiety about present, or even regret or shame about the past. This is done conscouosly by a few people, but done sub-consciously by most of the people. At times, depression or stress causes obcessive compulsive disorder where, one ends up in seeing only the darker side of eveything while ignoring the bright one.

In short, negative thinking has a very bad effect on almost every aspect of our actual life. A person with negative thinking not only makes his or her own outlook towards life negative, but also turns people around him or her negative towards life.

The common emotions nurtured by negativity are, anger, fear, restlessless and hopelessness. All these emotions increase stress of a person and have adverse effect on his life, success, relationships as well as health. They in turn end up in damaging the mind-frames as well as health of people having such mind frames and also people around them.

Such attitudes always come in the way of goal reaching ability as when one has a negative attitude, unknowingly, such a person pushes away everything that is likely to help us in reaching our goals.

Negative attitudes damage our health, lower our self-esteem, reduce our confidence, reduce our general energy level, and spoil our mood.

Effects of negative thinking can be listed as follows:

The primary reason to let go of negative thoughts is that they prevent you from enjoying all the benefits of positive thinking.

Once this is clear to your brain, it is more motivated and energized to help you take steps to stop thinking negatively. And this is how you start eliminating negative thinking on autopilot.

With this in mind, here are 11 effects of negative thinking, which are also 11 ways that negative thinking prevents you from enjoying the benefits of positive thinking.

1. Less worthwhile life
2. Less confidence
3. Lower self esteem
4. Less happiness and enjoyment
5. Less feelings of strength
6. Less energy
7. Less peace of mind
8. Less success instead of more success
9. Less enjoyable social interactions
10. Less health benefits
11. Less clarity of mind: since you have a choice, it doesn't make sense to think in negative ways that hurt you rather than positive ways that help you.

Let us see how and why this happens:

1. **A less worthwhile life instead of a more worthwhile life:** when a person is negative in his attitude, he makes his own life appear worthless or less worthwhile to people around him, thereby reducing his own value.
2. **Less confidence instead of greater confidence:** A negative person kills his own confidence & also provokes people to distrust himself due to his incapability expression.
3. **Lower self esteem instead of higher self esteem:** Self esteem is image about oneself in one's mind. A negative person has a poor image about himself in his mind due to his effort of generating sympathy and support.
4. **Less happiness and enjoyment instead of more happiness and enjoyment:** A negative person cannot enjoy life as a normal person. He creates sadness everywhere.
5. **Less feelings of strength instead of greater feelings of strength:** A negative person always keeps feeling weak and helpless, and makes others believe he is actually weak and helpless.
6. **Less energy instead of more energy:** A negative person always has no energy to do anything, however important it may be.
7. **Less peace of mind instead of more peace of mind:** A negative person is chronic restless. He also spreads this restlessness.
8. **Less success instead of more success:** A negative person is a universal looser. He kills his own success opportunities.
9. **Less enjoyable social interactions instead of more enjoyable social interactions:** Social interactions with a negative person are always depressing, so, people generally avoid a negative person.

10. **Less health benefits instead of more health benefits:** A negative attitude generates appearance of many health issues. This irritates people around a person.
11. **Less clarity of mind instead of greater clarity of mind: since you have a choice, it doesn't make much sense to think in negative ways that hurt you rather than positive ways that help you:** A negative person is always confused, makes wrong choices & motivates others to blame him.

Of course, knowing of all these effects of negative thinking is necessary for finding out various effects that influence our own life knowingly or unknowingly and once we spot the negative influences on it, then, releasing those negative impacts and turning all aspects of our life into positive one in order to achieve all-round progress, success and happiness in life.

CHAPTER XXXVI

Negative attitude and life

Life gets damaged in many ways due to negative attitude, and at the same time, the negative attitude also damages relationships of and around a negative person.

When we have a egative attitude, we are anyways damagig our life, but also when we are entertaining any person or group with negative attitudes, indirectly, we are supporting that negative attitude, accepting that negative attitude and damaging various aspects of our own life, health and success just by entertaining a negative attitude of a negative person.

This means, just as a positive attitude enriches our life, negative attitude impoverishs our life.

It is necessary to understand that our life becomes poor, stressful, unsuccessful, sad, not because of lack of opportunities, or by the emergence of sudden calamities in life, or by trouble given by others or by the jealousy or enmity that others have for us.

It becomes so, just because we feel defeated and accept the dark side of all such events as the only side of these events. Instead, when we start seeing the other brighter side, all the losses we suffer in life due to these so called things like lack of opportunities, sudden calamities, trouble or jealousy or enmity by others just vanish and our life starts getting enriched even in the most adverse situations.

Remember, negative attitude does not spoil the life. Actually it is our unpreparedness to handle the negative attitudes or situations is the real cause of losses we suffer due to negative attitudes.

CHAPTER XXXVII

Negative Personality Types:

There are certain types of people that indulge into negative states of mind. These are known as negativity prone personality types. They are all different in some ways of thinking and acting, but the unifying feature of all of them is their constant negativity. Each type of negative person has different ways of creating negativity & spreading it.

Some spread negativity so tactfully that people around never realize the negativity behind their behavior till they actually experience a major setback in their life. On the other hand, some people are openly negative and so, as soon as they start with their speech or reaction, their negativity is evident. We can list the negative personality types into eleven main categories as follows:

1. Miserable type
2. Silent killer type
3. Drama queen type
4. Woe is me type
5. Paranoid type
6. Trigger type
7. People Pleaser type
8. Active Aggressor or Violent type
9. Passive Aggressor or Manipulator type
10. Baby type
11. Negator type

Let's see the eleven negative types in details:

1. Miserable type

Such people present themselves as miserable right from beginning of the day. They meet with failures as soon as they wake up. This sets their day as a day full of anger and hopelessness. Usually such people are introvert types. Their presence makes others feel upset or moody. We can instantly feel their bad energy and must try to stay away from them. When we talk to people of this type, they easily insult us without even realizing it. This is because their negativity is so aligned with their being that they cannot recognize if they make others happy or sad.

The most interesting distinction of this type is that they are mainly unaware of their own mental state. They don't realize that they are negative. Friendship with such miserable people can make us seriously depressed. This is because they have a very strong negative energy resonating from within them which draws their near and dear ones into it and ruins them. Especially those who are mentally weak or insecure can easily become victims of such miserable types. In short, having such a person in our friends or family is dangerous as it invites misery to us. So we must either be away from such person or we must handle him and his attitude effectively.

2. Silent killer

Silent killer type of people understand human as well as animal psychology quite well. They use this knowledge of psychology to gradually introduce slow poison of hatred, anger and low self-esteem in people around them.

They do it simply by passing casual looking remarks about how others behave or look. They know very well that their remarks are destructive, but they always take care that others around them do not realize that these remarks damage or destroy these people around them.

For example, our friend casually implies that we should not wear this type of dress because it emphasizes some part of our body. We must see the real intention behind the advice. It is actually a way to make us conscious for no reason. At times, when we meet dream partner and both are in love with each other. We meet this negative friend and start conversation about our dream partner. The friend makes such remark: 'Hmm, I wonder what made her choose you...' This kind of statements make us question our appearance and abilities and leads to low self-esteem and self-doubt. The reason why silent killers act this way is because they are very insecure beings. Because of that, they want to make others feel as insecure as them. Getting others in such negative state gives them reassurance, control and satisfaction.

3. Drama queen

This isthe most common type of negative attitude. Since this type of negative attitude is very loud, in most of the dramas and films, the characters express emotions this way. This is the reason why the name Drama Queen has been given to this type of attitudes. Most of the times, females exhibit this attitude, so the word queen and not the king. Had the case been reverse and if there were more men exhibiting this type of attitude, it would have been called a 'Drama King' instead of 'Drama Queen'!

Their emotions range from anger to self-pity. They have a potential to turn any small incident into storm. They seem to like the fact that they can change the feelings of others and stay as the centres of attention.They are chronic are needy and insecure, they crave for constant reassurance. They strive for attention and approval. If they don't receive what they want, they act childish. They start crying, throwing things around or trying to get on others' nerves.

Of course, this behaviour eventually backfires on them. Once that happens, drama queens become scared and surprised by the reaction they caused. This way drama queens try to make others feel guilty and cruel. This kind of behavior is the result of neediness and low self esteem.

4. *Woe is me*

People of this negative type love to talk about their failures to everyone. In a way they are extensions of the miserable type of people. They don't just express their incapability, but they show it off. They do that purely to get attention and sympathy of others. They are incapable heroes! To these people, describing deeds of failure and narrating them with utmost interest is an act of heroism. Such people relish their incapability and project to children and weaker ones around that failure and incapability is something to be spoken about, to be proud of and to be relished! Many people do not realize that narrating such unfortunate stories can do a lot of harm.

Those who wish to succeed in life should stay away from such people because such people draw others into their imagined world of unfairness and unhappiness. They narrate that the actual reality of the world is unhappiness and unfairness.

Weak and ignorant people or people who have never seen the world, believe in them and then they can never succeed in life. This type of people specially affect the minds of weak people. By listening to the stories of the 'woe is me' type, one is likely to start visualizing their troubles and invite them into your own life.

5. The paranoid type

These people always insecure, scared and suspect danget or threat. They feel that others are constantly trying to harm them. Even when they go for shopping, they keep thinking that shopkeeper is trying to cheat on them.

If anyone is friendly with them, they think that such a person wants something from them. Once they encounter one unfortunate situation when they are treated unfairly, they start seeing unfairness everywhere. It may come to the stage where they would see that everyone is against them.

This type is characterized by pervasive, universal suspiciousness & generalized mistrust. Such individuals are hypersensitive, easily feel slighted, and habitually relate to the world by vigilant scanning of the environment for clues or suggestions that validate their fear or bias.

Paranoid individuals are eager observers. They think they are in danger and look for signs and threats of that danger, potentially not appreciating other evidence. They tend to be guarded and suspicious and have quite constricted emotional lives.

People of this type may or may not have a tendency to bear grudges, suspiciousness, tendency to interpret others' actions as hostile, persistent tendency to self-reference, or a tenacious sense of personal right. This negative attitude is mainly caused by self-doubt and poor self-image.

6. Trigger type

Trigger type of people are insecure and full of inferiority complex. They always look for opportunities to get upset and release the inner volcano of dissatisfaction of someone or other. People of this personality type seek ways to release their anger or self-pity.

It appears that there is an active volcano within them that is always looking or a smallest opportunity for it to irupt. Then their irruption becomes violent or full of drama or full of tears depending on the type of volcano that is active within the being of such a person. They are always in search of minutest spark to set the volcano alive.

Such people often get into conversation in such a way that they provoke others to feel angry or hopeless, get into a heated argument with them, make them aggressive, create a scene and in turn destroy their mental balance and health.

At times they spark an argument and start accusing someone of doing something insignificant and continues with accusations until the other person finally breaks down & reacts in way that triggers them. By releasing their emotions they release their own negativity. When they emit negative emotions, they give some of their negative energy to the people they argue with.

This means the way in which a trigger type person spreads negativity is, either by getting triggered or by making others get triggered. The emotional blasts created by such triggers emit negativity that stays for long and ruins many things and relations and opportunities in life. So, it is better to keep away at safe distance from trigger type persons. We must start creating and maintaining it as soon as we locate or suspect a person to be of a trigger type.

7. People Pleaser Type

The People Pleaser types try to find their self-worth through constantly doing things for other people. It's nice to do things for others, but cannot be a way to survive. Yet, this type of people need the happines of people in order to survive. They can go to any extent whatsoever in order to keep others happy.

People pleaser types feel worthless if they have no people around or if people around are not happy by their actions. The People Pleaser's motivation is not generosity but need of validation & recognition, allowing them to feel like they're worth something.

When the People Pleaser doesn't receive the validation and attention they believe they're entitled to, resentment can set in, and they blame others for not appreciating them. Then they feel worse about themselves, and try to fix this feeling by pleasing again. This becomes a never-ending cycle of pleasing.

People Pleasers actually have a very poor self esteem. So, they need to establish their own worth in their own mind by getting recognition. For this, they feel the need to be taken advantage of and then being appreciated. This is how the trait starts in first place. They establish relationships of imbalance in give and take where people with whom they get related, take too much and too often.

Generally if this happens with any normal person, one always gently puts one's foot down and push the advantage seekers away without even making them realize so. But people pleasers never do so. People Pleasers need to learn to concentrate on themselves and their own lives, and to not find their identity in others.

8. Active Aggressor or Violent Type

There are two basic types of aggression; ***overt-aggression*** and ***covert-aggression***. Overt aggression is active aggression where a person uses violent physical power with tantrums while covert aggression is passive aggression where one uses tactics that manipulate.

When one is determined to do something and when one is open about it, his violent behaviour is direct and obvious. Such behaviour is overtly or openly and clearly aggressive. Generally people exhibiing such aggression regularly are called as terrirosm spreading characters in society if such agression is regularly exhibited by any person.

Aggressor is a type who exhibits aggression in such a way that it can put us off and generate a feeling of fear in us. The Aggressor uses blatant tactics to get what they need. They try to make it obvious to the world that they can do anything. They use intimidation hostility bossiness etc. People often allow the Aggressor to get their way because it's easier to avoid confrontation than suffer their wrath. The Aggressor is an angry person who always needs to prove to the world that he is right.

Underneath this active aggressor, there is a person who is defeated from within. At times, in such a person, there is a person, who, as a child was on the receiving end of the type of behavior he now shows. That means, an aggressor knows that he is weak, he has no power. If he does not exhibit aggression, people will never give him what he wants, because he does not deserve what he wants. We must avoid arguing with Aggressor if we really wish to be strong.

9. Passive Aggressor or Manipulator Type

When one is out to "win" dominate or control but is subtle, underhanded or deceptive enough to hide one's true intentions, the behaviour is covertly or passively aggressive. This type of aggression not only helps a person dominate, but also keep his aggression under cover. While dominating in this way, one is never openly aggressive.

The Passive Aggressor or covert aggressor manipulates people deviously. They gain their false sense of power by taking shots at others. They often use disguised sarcasm as a joke to make people feel inferior about a quality that someone has. This is because in the sarcastic jokes, the passive aggressors pass some offensive remarks about some qualities of someone around them, and laugh at that person.

The passive aggressors will never be direct with criticism. They hide and mask themselves as more friendly than they really are. In hindi, such people are called "meethi churi". The Passive Aggressor needs to be reprimanded about their aggression, but we must do so very calmly, else they can make a fool of us in front of people due to their tactics. They need to be told that we are aware of what they are doing by trying to make us feel bad.

They are passing wrong remarks at us and that their behavior is totally unacceptable. They must behave themselves as these remarks are baseless and unnecessary, and passed in order to humiliate and insult us publically with intention. They will do anything to avoid confrontation and being centre stage, so being direct with them is how you counteract their behavior.

People with both active as well as passive types of aggression expect a reaction of intimidation. If we are not intimidated by their tactics, they feel defeated and back out.

So, we must be rational in our approach. When they get aggressive, we must look them in eye. We must never show weakness or fear. Our weakness makes an aggressor strong.

Both active and passive aggressors know it very well that they are weak, but they do not want the world to know about their weakness, so, if they are physically strong, they use physical violence or active aggression, and if they are not physically strong or if they do not want their aggression to be exposed, they use passive aggression in the form of manipulation. They know that they can never win with the help of logic and so, they use either violence or manipulation to get what they want.

10. Baby Type

Baby type person has a chroic baby like behaviour. They never act or react as adults, their gestures are always like a child. This is something that always taken as abnormal by peopple with whom such people deal with.

The Baby type person tends to see things in a negative light. Such people are centered on their own self. They use the defence mechanism of regression when they get into difficult situation. When no one listens to them, and they have no way to convince logically, they cry and complain to get their way. They act like cranky babies and throw tantrums to get attention of people around.

Though every person has a baby within, the danger of interacting with the Baby types is that while interacting with them, our inner baby may be engaged as well and we may start reacting like babies as well without realizing it. So, we must be careful that we never agree with the Baby's whining and complaining.

We must logically show the bright side of things and dismiss a negative dialogue, ignoring the negative attitudes completely, while dealing with baby type personalities.

We must openly speak up make the baby type people realize that they are grown ups and not small babies. Such verbal confrontation keeps our inner baby safe and our inner baby does not get trapped in the tantrums these persons throw to get their things done in their way.

We can see that people who have never succeeded in life, i.e. chronic looser types are the ones who exhibit this personality quite often. It is actually an excessive use of the defence mechanism of regression.

Defence mechanism is our sub-conscious mind process of face saving that tries to keep us away from shock. Of course, excessive use of any defence mechanism leads to deviation from reality and mental disorders.

In regression, in order to forget the present failure or unwanted events, one starts behaving like a child by mentaly going back to the period of life when these problems were not there.

11. Negator Type

The Negator does not accept anything positive because they have been let down badly in their earlier years. They distrust almost everyone, they are completely closed to suggestion, and they only see the cup as half empty. The Negator is the one who will tell you why something won't work; they will never offer a solution or encouragement.

Don't let your positive energy be sucked out by the Negator. Stay positive around them. Staying realistic and showing them the logical side of why things can work and can be good is the way to deal with them.

Inside, they want positivity, they're just afraid to risk the disappointment which characterized their childhoods. They would rather destroy something before it destroys them.

The key to dealing with these negative personalities is to not let yourself be pulled down to their level of behavior, and to maintain your own identity. All these behavioral traits are ways of getting attention and sign of insecurity.

We are actually dealing with a wounded child within them and not their true personality. Showing them mature behavior by example is the kindest and most productive way to help them.

These are common types of people with negative attitude. One person can have a mixture of several types, but then one type will be more prominent than others.

CHAPTER XXXVIII

Changing negative attitude to positive

When we say that positive attitude is needed for good life, we must see how we can shift attitude of anyone else or of our own self, when we are negative. Remeevery coin has two sides and so does every event or stuation. It is possible to change negative attitude into positive, but it is noteasy. If you lived your life seeing only dark side of life, you cannot shift this way of seeing just in a day. It takes time. However, by taking small and consistent steps you will gradually become a happier person.

The best way to change your mental state is by understanding the outcome of negativity. Carefully read the consequences of negative attitude and they will serve as reminders as soon as your mood goes down. You will think twice before getting upset, angry or depressed.

You cause your own mood and you can change it by simply focusing on good aspects of your life or imagining something positive. You are not at the mercy of different kinds of negative feelings that visit you when you least expect. You can control how you feel.

As soon as you spot a negative aspect of a situation or thing, try your best to find its positive aspect instead. For example, if you oversleep, you think that you will be late for work. Instead try to find what you gain from over-sleeping. You may realise that your efficiency will increase significantly because of the extra hours of sleep.

Always look at the positive aspects of any situation that you find yourself in. This will boost your spirit and you will start turning positive in every situation you come across.

You should try to understand what causes your negative attitude. It might be that you live with a person who constantly ruins your mood or it may also be something to do with your past. Maybe something happened to you that made you deeply upset and you have not recovered from that incident since.

Try to understand that when the incident is long gone, you should not live in the shadow of it. Your past can only have influence on your present if you let it. Remember, your whole power is in the present moment.

Positive thinking is not enough. If you cannot find the cause of your negative attitude, you will only cover this attitude with positive words which will do no good to you. So try to find the cause of it and this will allow you to change your negative attitude.

Sometimes causes are internal rather than external. In fact, any external cause will lead you to the deeper, internal cause. For example, you might understand that you are negative because your family makes you negative. But when you dig deeper, you may realize that you feel unworthy as a person and you project this unworthiness onto your family and that makes you angry at them. It's true that the qualities you don't like in other people are yours, so it's not others that are at fault but you. So in this example you uncover that it's your limiting belief of unworthiness that makes you negative. The next step will be to eliminate it and then your attitude will improve.

Digging deep within will help you find what pricks you and what maks see the dark side. Once you do it, wrthe wound and things will start turning beautiful. This is a simple way to turn a negative mindet into positive, but for sure, it is no , especially when we are working oelves. This is because, w tendency to deny things that hurt us.

Negative attitude serves no good to you or others. The quicker you start changing, the sooner you'll notice the benefits. People will start treating you differently and you'll notice opportunities wherever you go. You'll start seeing the world as full of happiness and possibilities. From now on, start planting the seeds of joy, love and happiness. This will pave your way to success in everything you do.

When we use the mental level delineations, the minds of these masters also send their support to give more power to manifest our intention. Then, the speed with which the intention materialises into reality increases to a great extent. Also these delineations refer to the mental processes of the healer or healed ones.

CHAPTER XXXIX

Mind work for Active empowerment

To empower our mind, we must first locate and handle the thoughts that limit us.

Most of the times, our own thoughts block our success and we blame others for it.

So, active mind work for empowerment is absolutely necessary before we proceed on the mind level of Vishitao.

Here is an exercise for this:

Find out and list out the things that you want to heal in your life. Write down these wishes as you would write them after they are completed. Imagine your desires as if you are seeing them as fulfilled.

Do these exercises for 10 desires in your life.

1. Read your wishes carefully
2. Locate the thoughts that are stopping you
3. Wish to release blocking thoughts.
4. Mentally cut chords with blocking thoughts.
5. Feel that all mental, blocks are released.
6. Use *kshed* on energy ball and place it on the naval if you feel that support is needed.
7. Feel that all emotional blocks are released.
8. Feel that all spiritual blocks are released.
9. Feel confident to manifest your desires.
10. Get up and start routine.

With the delineations on the energy field the speed at which it manifests our desires increases to a great extent. Let us see delineations of this level:

CHAPTER XL

1. Megi - courage:

Megi is one of the simplest and yet one of the most powerful delinations.

The way of drawing it is very simple, so, anyone can use it easily while using Vishitao.

Here we use just two colours.

To draw Megi, we first draw an orange circle.

Orange is the colour of strength.

Then we draw a florescent green curved sleeping reverse 's' in the centre of it.

Green is the colour of healing love.

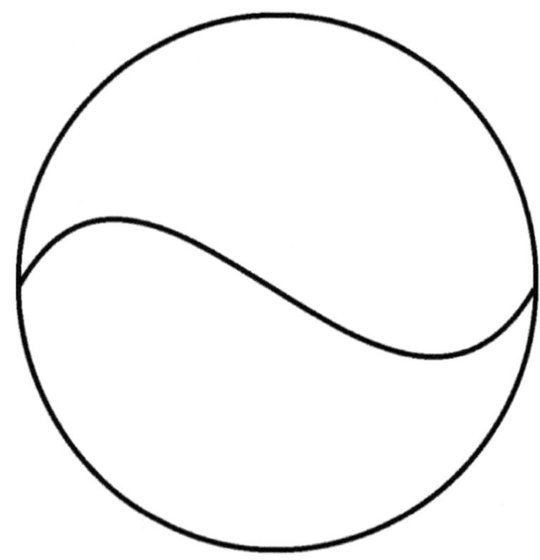

Megi

This is how we draw Megi to install courage in persons to whomwe are sending healing.

Megi is courage delineation.

Mind has a tendency to get depressed easily.

So, we must remember that in difficulty or while handling difficult situation, courage is a must.

This delineation helps us to generate the required amount of courage.

We may use it for ourselves or for anyone who needs courage.

At times, a patient loses the drive to get healed. In such situations too we may use this delineation and help him have the necessary courage to get well.

For using this, we must see the person in energy field and send the field with this delineation on it.

CHAPTER XLI

2. Som - Intuition:

Som is the delination for enhancing our intuition.

Whenever we are working on any situation, we need to develop a perfect insight about the things we wish to manifest.

This needs an accurate intuition that Som gives us.

The delination Som can be drawn in two possible ways.

One is in black & white colour.

The other is in indigo & golden colours.

The black or indigo in left indicates dark past.

The white or golden in right indicates bright future.

Neither part of life is fully dark or bright.

So there is a dot of white in black and black in white.

Som helps us to stay balanced at all times.

Som

The help of intuition is needed in some situations in order to be able to deal with them better.

We may use it for ourselves or for anyone whom we wish to help getting right intuitions.

The signals that we get after this delineation are like some strong thoughts in the mind.

This delineation is used by visualizing the person needing intuitions in the energy field and then drawing this delineation over the field and releasing.

It may even be used for groups of people who need to think in the right way.

CHAPTER XLII

3. Stroc - breaking barriers:

Stroc is drawn with regular & inverted slanting 'w's.
These are fluorescent green in colour.
These are upward in left and downward in right side.
They are intersecting each other
As they do this, they form 3 connected parallelograms.
The free line endings create X look at both ends.
The parallelograms have light purple circles inside them.
On left side of these, we draw a dark pink slanting line.
This is in left upward & in right side downward.

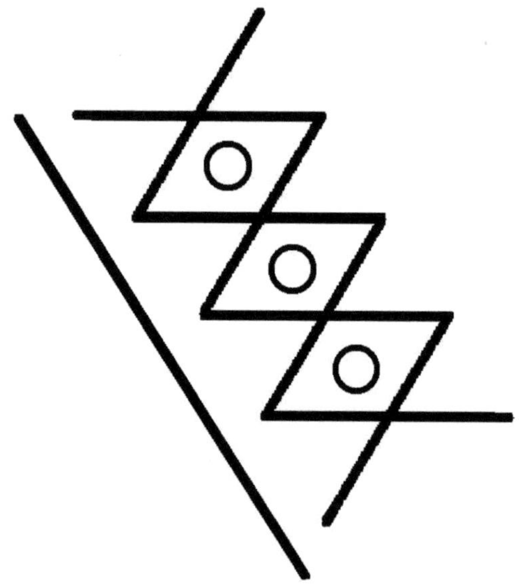

Stroc

Stroc is a delination for breaking barriers.

Mind is like a mokey and is prone to create blocks and barriers in everything it creates.

To project or receive the energies mind must be free from blocks and barriers.

The mind blocks and barriers are formed in the sub-conscious level of mind.

This is the reason why we are generally not aware of blocks present in our own mind.

Unless all conscious and sub-conscious barriers are released, energies cannot work.

Stroc helps us release both conscious and subconscious blocks & barriers.

So wherever we are working on everything, make a practice to use stroc after the first two delineations.

The energies will be both sent and received better.

We may use it even for ourselves.

CHAPTER XLIII

4. Megrow - Increase:

Megrow is a growth delination.
We see a wide range of colours in this delination.
The first part, i.e. '7' of megrow is dark purple.
It indicates rising of strength.
The second line, the sleeping '7' is indigo on colour.
It indicates reduction of weakness.
Then the curved '^' in sky blue is drawn.
It indicates manifesting of divine will.
Then we draw golden green 'n'.
This indicates protected landing of this divine will.
Below that, we draw curved 'v' in dark green
This indicates the process of rooting this event.
At the end, we draw sleeping '7' in red.
It brings firm grounding of manifestation of divine will.
This is how we draw Megrow.

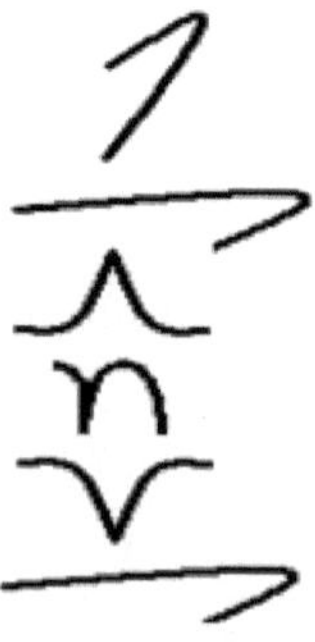

Megrow

It is to be used to produce any kind of growth.

This growth is both at physical as well as mental level.

Megrow can be used to increase any emotion or activity of mind, body, event or for speeding up spiritual growth.

It may even be used to increase abundance, healing, harmony, good relation etc.

Basically, to make anything grow faster and better, Megrow can be used.

When we wish to use this delineation visualize the event we wish to create or increase.

Draw all other delineations necessary and then draw Megrow to make the visualized event grow faster and then draw Hon Sui for rooting and send.

CHAPTER XLIV

5. Melow - decrease:

Melow is a delination of decrease.
We see a blue family of colours in this delination.
To draw melow, we first draw a sleeping light purple '7'.
It indicates reduction related divine will.
Then we draw sky blue straight vertical line.
On both sides of this, we draw two sky blue / & \ lines.
So we form a sky blue '/|\'.
This indicate reduction energies directed to divine will.
Then we draw dark blue horizontal line.
This indicates landing of reduction energies.
Below that we draw '7' and reverse of '7' in dark blue.
This indicates grounding of reduction energies.
Then we draw a dark purple 'm' below it.
It indicates fixation of this reduction with divine will.

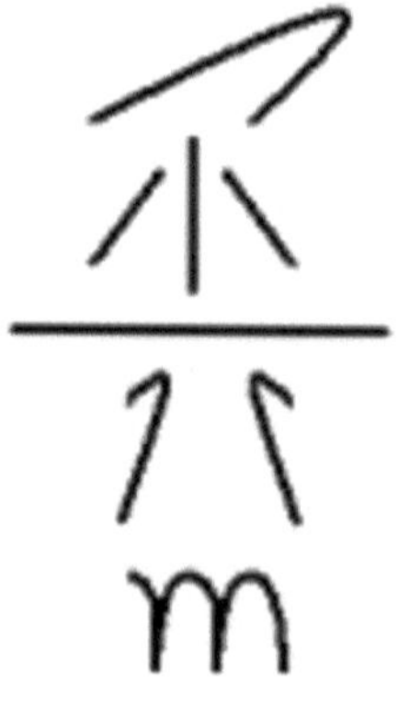

Melow

This delineation is useful in creating & manifesting i.e. producing reduction.

We can use it to decrease and reduce anything like abscess, or tumour or growth of viruses or the skin problems like pimples etc.

When we are using this delineation we must visualize the event or area where we need to produce reduction clearly, put it in the energy field and draw this delineation and send.

While using mellow it is advisable to use other supporting delineations as well.

CHAPTER XLV

6. Chi Hon Swe - total harmony:

Chi Hon swe is a colourful symbol of total harmony.
To draw Chi Hon Swe, we begin with a purple diamond.
It represents the glow of divine will.
Then we draw yellow circle,
This indicates the power of divine will.
Below it, we draw purple curved '^'.
It has a small vertical purple line inside it.
This indicates the process of landing of this divine will.
Then we draw a baby pink inverted box.
It has two parallel vertical dark pink '=' ilines inside it.
This is a process of establishing affectionate harmony.
Then we draw horizontal green line below the box.
Then we draw two golden green '7's on both its sides.
It shows grounding & growing of affectionate harmony.
Then we draw a brown zigzag line below it.
It indicates strengthening of this grounding.
Below it, we draw a sky blue wavy line.
This shows water-body below strengthening factor.
It indicates nurturing of the grounding.
Then we draw a dark pink 'x'
It has small red circles at ends of all four line endings.
This indicates the speeding up of this whole process.
This is how we draw Chi Hon swe.

This delineation is useful in producing a total harmony in our physical, mental as well as spiritual level.

It balances the energies of the body, mind and soul in order to give complete stability to a person.

Chi Hon Swe

We may use this delineation for creating and restoring total harmony.

Even in establishing or restoring harmony in events, groups and places, this is useful.

It is advisable to use this delineation after rest of the healing work is done.

This means, when we finish with drawing other delineations, we can use this one.

This is because, with it, we complete the incompletion left by other delineations.

This helps us to create total harmony in the real sense.

CHAPTER XLVI

Practice needed by Mental level healer

When we use the delineations of mental level, we work on the minds of people we are healing.

At the same time, we receive greater support from the minds of divine masters in our healing.

So in both ways our healing is powerful.

The support of divine minds is available with this level.

So when we are initiated to the mental level of Vishitao, we get greater force in our healing irrespective of delineations we are using.

Then divine minds support is with we as a healer.

When a mental level healer practices, he can work on the mind as well as on the basic and material levels of the persons as well as events.

A Mental level healer can follow the following steps in healing:

- Always begin with Vishitao and Kemizap and end with Polora.
- For healing purpose, use Reymzen with the required other delineations
- For getting abundance, use Hon Sui, Ri Mega, Megi, som and megrow.
- For event creation, use Metra, Swe som and chi hon swe.
- In case if one finds obstacles in events, use stroc to release them.
- For healing relations, use Reymzen, Som, O tu se or Awem, Hon Sui and chi hon swe.

- For reducing heat in atmosphere around, use sil with melow
- For reducing coldness around, use Grim with megrow
- For removing wrong things around, first protect good people with polora and then by creating next energy field, send Kshed, stroc, melow and swe on wrong things.
- To remove bad habits or thoughts in people around, visualize bad habit or thought in them and then, draw kshed and stroc.
- For improving memory and decision-making power, use Som, Megrow and chi hon swe.
- We may think of many more delineation combinations like this.
- Vishitao seekers at mental level may certainly visualize many more combinations
- They can also share and discuss these new combos with other vishitao seekers.
- Also, after or while learning the VISHITAO at this level,
- When you think of or see some new combinations, please feel free to share them with us by sending a whatsapp message on 9820044254 or 9870044254.
- This will help us to see ti it that those things can be incorporated in our next edition of this book.

Later on after doing the next two levels, it is possible to use these delineations in combination with the delineations of those levels that would make the work more powerful.

SPIRITUAL LEVEL

1. Spiritual level
2. Protecting as a master
3. Qualities of a master
4. Abilities of a master
5. Cautions needed for a master
6. Posture attitude & vocabulary for a master
7. Active introspection
8. Cleaning blocks
9. Active divination
10. Adichi
11. Detra
12. La zen
13. Ta chi
14. Redizen
15. Diagnosis & scanning

CHAPTER XLVII

Spiritual level

This level helps us to get help and support from the divine spiritual readers of the highest level.

It also accelerates our own spiritual growth.

Methods to be used at spiritual level during the process of healing as a master:

At spiritual level, a master learns scanning that helps to know problem area that we needs healing. But just this much does not let us heal as a master. There are many other things that we must do as a master when we heal.

Let us see which these things are:

1: Checking patient's resistance level: Healing is obstructed most of the times due to the resistance a patient has towards getting well.

Many times a person says that he wants to come out of a situation, but actually, he is happy within with the pay-off that he is getting out of that problem.

So he does not want to let go of the pay-off and yet, to satisfy his ego, or to fulfill the social demands, he says that he wants to get rid of the problem.

At such times, it is the duty of the master to check if it is worth releasing the resistance or it is better to let the person be with the problem.

2: Checking our gut feeling: This is when a master has to check his gut feeling.

When a master finds anything or person that needs healing, he must keep his hands on his naval and check the energy he feel there.

This helps a master know his inner attitude towards the person or event or thing to be healed as well as the signals masters are giving about healing that thing.

3: Releasing blocks in patient: if the master feels that he must release the blocks within the patient about healing, the master must begin with that first.

It is only after this is done, a master must start with actual scanning and healing of problem narrated by patient.

4: Checking of the possibility of reoccurrence of problem: Evenwhen we have healed the problem as a master, we find that after a while, the problem appears again.

This happens not just in case of healing with Vishitao and other spiritual sciences, but also happens in case of treatments with universally recognized and accepted methods.

This especially happens in ailments like cancer that relapses a few years after chemotherapy or surgery.

So, when a Vishitao master heals from master level, he must check the possibility of relapse before finally declaring that the patient is healed.

If he finds the possibility of relapse, he must continue the healing for some more time so that the possibility of relapse is pushed away.

Yet, in some cases, a master must also advice the patient to learn Vishitao himself at least till second level and keep healing himself at least twice a week.

CHAPTER XLVIII

Protecting as a master

At spiritual level, one becomes a master and gets the ability to protect and heal as master.

To heal effectively as well as to know about threats around a person, one scans the patient.

Scanning helps us know the problem area and heal it quickly and effectively.

But when healing is done, there is a possibility that the negative energies that are released from the system of a patient during the healing process; may get attracted back into the system of a patient in some time.

This happens if the patient attracts the negativity himself or if some near and dear person of the patient attracts it due to his worry for the patient.

At time if the negative energy has some inner power to re-enter the aura of the patient, it comes back and produces the problem again.

Yet in any such case, a patient of Vishitao Master can stay protected from this possibility if master keeps him under Vishitao protection shield for 24 hours till he gives the next healing session to the patient.

There is a powerful technique that a Vishitao healer at spiritual level can use to protect his patients.

Here a master sets a pection shield around the patient.

For doing this, a master must do a very simple thing after healing is done.

Of course, shield must be created only after conclusively finding that the energies in and around the patient are now in perfect place.

Following are steps for a protection shield:

1. Visualize a transparent ball of fluorescent green light.
2. Visualize the patient inside that ball.
3. Visualize a cover of indigo colour around this ball.
4. Visualize a cover of violet flame
5. Place it around this indigo shield.
6. Visualize a cover of golden light
7. Place it around the violet flame.
8. Visualize golden light emitting Fluorescent Green flame.
9. Visualise the golden light emitting Violet flame around.
10. Let patient be inside this structure.
11. Keep him there till next healing session.

Once a master protects a patient this way, a master can ensure that released negatives are not back in the patient.

This makes the healing by a master very effective and people healed by a master get better results.

Ideally, a Vishitao master must protect his patient this way after every healing session so that the healing given by him has a lasting effect.

After a number of daily healing sessions in a difficult case, a master may keep such a shield even for a week or so.

He may keep doing this even for a while when the patient has become relatively stable and is out of danger.

CHAPTER XLIX

Qualities of a master

On becoming a master, one develops a few qualities. these are unique to masterhood of any discipline.

This means any master of any spiritual methodology develops all these qualities in himself.

Nobody teaches these qualities.

They simply start unfolding from within when the master unfolds from within a person.

Of course, this is not a process of a few hours or days. It is a slow process and slowly and steadily this starts happening.

- **Master has total control over himself.**

This means, a master can control bodily demands so effectively, that at times, others do not even realise those demands. For example, of one feels hungry at a place where no food is available, master just gives Vishitao to his stomach and his hunger is taken care of, and no one even knows that he was hungry!

- **Master sees no difference in self & others**

Master is a person without double standards. A double standard is having one rule for oneself & other for others. Master has the same rules for himself & others; there is no difference between himself & others. So whatever is right for himself is right for all, & whatever is wrong for himself is wrong for all in his eyes.

- **Master is one with the surroundings.**

He can adjust in any situation in the best possible way. A master has no adjustment problems and so blends well everywhere. As a result, a master generally is so transparent that people may find it difficult to differentiate him from any other ordinary person. The only difference between an ordinary person and a master is that a master never complains, he is never unhappy or uncomfortable in any situation whatsoever.

- **Master is in total control of thoughts emotions & desires in his mind.**

A master is fully in control while experiencing as well as expressing emotion as he has this basic knowledge, that losing control over yourself is giving your strings in the hands of others. These others are the ones due to whom the emotion is generated. Once you give your strings in the hands of others, you just become a puppet and then others may take any type of undue advantage of you! A master never lets this happen. He is always in control of himself.

- **Master can make a positive difference in the life of others just by his being.**

At times, just the presence of a master is enough to heal the person or situation. This is because; the aura of a master is so strong that once anyone enters it, he gets healed.

CHAPTER L

Abilities of a master

A master is never born.

Nor is a master created by learning.

Once a person develops necessary awareness, the master starts unfolding from within him.

When after master healer's training, a healer starts practicing with full dedication, this process begins.

This time some of the qualities mentioned below start appearing in a healer in some degrees, but only when the master is fully unfolded, these qualities are seen in constant and consistent way in a master.

Once this happens fully, we can see a specific set of abilities in such a master.

These are the abilities we can see in a fully evolved master of any discipline.

- **A master can scan a patient and find out the area of problem. He can do so by mentally seeing aura or scanning it with his hands.**

In master level of healers training, one learns to scan a patient or a situation and find out the problem area. Once he learns this, he heals much faster as now he knows what & how much to heal.

- **A master can detect the emotion involved in the ailment from observation of symptoms of the patient.**

A master learns to read, understand and effectively use the chart of emotions and body parts connected with them to know the emotions behind any ailment.

- **A master can heal thoughts and emotions of a patient.**

Once a master knows about the emotions involved in the ailment, he can use effective counseling along with Vishitao to remove the emotions from the mind of the patient and also he heals the thoughts by using mental method of healing. He knows that 99.99 ailments have a psycho-somatic origin. So along with the body, mind also has to be healed for a permanent recovery.

- **A master can create desire in patient to heal himself.**

At times, the patient just has no will to get well. Patient just thinks that his ailment is not curable and that he will stay sick forever. He also thinks that no one can help him. This makes the patient keep on pulling back ill health even in spite of repeated healing done by many healers over a long period of time. In such cases; Master uses counselling as well as mental method of healing to create this desire in a patient and give him mental strength to get well.

- **A master has detached attachment with patient.**

As a master has detached attachment, he just works to prepare a patient to deserve the healing. He does not expect anything. He knows that once a patient deserves good health, he is going to get it without any difficulty. This means, though he monitors the healing, he does not have any anxiety about the healing speed of a patient.

CHAPTER LI

Cautioons needed for a master

Being a master is a state of great responsibility. One wrong or irresponsible action done by a master has a potential to create a great damage, so, a master must take a few cautions while doing anything in life.

- **A master must not use intentions irresponsibly.**

If a master intends things without thinking properly, and gives Vishitao to these intentions, even if the intention is not appropriate, still, the intentions may come true. Then the master may repent. A master must remember that unlike in Vishitao 2, where Vishitao takes care of your intentions and manifests ONLY things that are good for you, when a Vishitao master intends anything, Vishitao just supports the desire of a master and follows it unconditionally.

- **A master must avoid losing temper.**

If a master loses his temper, he may say things which may harm someone, and with his power, those things may come true. Afterwards, he may repent. So, he must be very careful now.

- **A master must avoid irresponsible comments and judgments. He must know that he has to be a witness and not a judge.**

A master must remember that he is just a witness. He must not judge things. On judging, if he passes some irresponsible comments, they may be improper to his image as a master and at the same time, they may also prove to be harmful to him or others at times.

- **A master must avoid EMOTIONAL INVOLVEMENT with patient. His attachment may delay the healing process of the patient.**

If a master is emotionally attached with the patient, he may also have fear of failure at the back of his mind. This may come in the way of the healing of the patient and healing may get delayed.

- **A master must avoid making negative statements that are assertive as his power may make them true. Then he may repent.**

If a master passes any negative assertive comments or makes any negative assertive statement, his power may bring them into reality. If he feels later that he did a mistake, may be he will not be in a position to create a contrary event by that time. So he has to be careful about saying things.

CHAPTER LII

Posture, attitude, & vocabulary for a master

A master must be careful in using words as using wrong vocabulary may give wrong signals to the patients and others with whom a master is speaks.

At no point of time must a master indicate that he has some supernatural powers.

Master must never indicate that others are poor in awareness as compared to him.

Master must be humble in attitude and expression.

Master must live the Vishitao principles in real sense and must never express any kind of anxiety or aggression or anger.

Master must never indicate any disrespect to any one in any way whatsoever.

At times, behavior of someone deserves to invite disrespect or contempt.

Yet, master must be respectful to such people. Master must be a living expression of gratitude and service.

This certainly does not mean that a master must keep doing charity at the cost of his own living.

If a master finds people around him expecting such a charity out of him, he must politely explain that charity is something that is to be done to those who really deserve charity.

Others must pay for the services of healing received out of master.

Master must always have a scientific, clear, respectful, polite, professional attitude where he gives respect and also maintains his own respect and space.

Even while scanning, master must never intrude the personal space of others as it is known as spiritual trace pass and though not taken as a crime on civil or criminal way, it is certainly a crime on spiritual plane.

So, a master must refrain from intrusion in the personal area of a patient.

If a master finds something personal about someone while scanning, he must never discuss it with patient in public.

He may request to talk to patient in privacy and then disclose his findings to the patient.

This helps the patient maintain his personal space.

Even when a master finds something conclusively negative about the condition of thought formations or of the past of patient, Master must never indicate that he has seen it so clearly.

Instead, he must politely ask the patient and let him talk of those negative memories.

By his soothing words, powerful posture and positively polite attitude, a master must always command respect of people around.

The divine Angels who are God's messengers and who are worshipped as Gods in different forms in different religions are the one who extend their help at this level.

That means the help that we receive here in our work is beyond mental level, from spiritual level of the existence.

To grow spiritually, we need to raise our spiritual level which is actually possible by perfect thinking and by right meditations.

Here are a few simple meditations that we can practice daily:

ACTIVE INTROSPECTION:

1. Sit peacefully
2. Take a pen and paper.
3. Write things you like about yourself.
4. Write what you feel about these things.
5. Write things you dislike about yourself.
6. Write what you feel about these things.
7. List the people whom you respect in life.
8. Write the reasons of this respect.
9. List the people whom you hate in life.
10. Write the reasons of this hatred.
11. List the people whom you miss in life.
12. Write reasons of missing these people.
13. List out people whom you want to forgive
14. Write the reasons for it
15. List people whom you wish to forgive you.
16. Write reasons for it
17. Keep thinking on all this & start routine

ACTIVE DIVINATION:

1. Sit in front of a mirror.
2. Look at yourself.
3. Keep watching yourself minutely.
4. Watch your thoughts while watching yourself.
5. Remember your favourite God or master.
6. Imagine that God or master inside your heart
7. Look in the mirror while imagining God within
8. Feel strong & powerful & start routine.

CLEANING BLOCKS:

1. Find some peaceful moments.
2. Start thinking while doing daily activities.
3. Remember past 10 similar obstacles you had.
4. Remember thoughts you had just before it.
5. Place your hand on naval & check your feeling.
6. Recognize the pattern of blocks in your life.
7. Remember thoughts about your helplessness.
8. Realize that helplessness caused these blocks
9. Consciously drop this helpless feeling.
10. Acknowledge your ability to succeed.
11. Feel free of all obstacles in life.
12. Start your life afresh

As soon as we are initiated for the spiritual level we start receiving this help. Then the energy field we create and energize becomes more powerful and gives faster results.

CHAPTER LIII

1. Adichi – divine light:

Let us see the delineations of this level:

The first Delination of this level is Adichi.

This delineation gives us increased power of healing.

This is a purple ten headed star.

It is drawn in continued lines.

They go clockwise.

To draw the star in Adichi, we first draw a purple vertical line in the left.

It is drawn from up to down.

Then we go up with slant towards right,

Then we come back crossing vertical line backwards.

Then we go up again, with a slant upwards towards right,

Then we draw a vertical line parallel to the first one.

Then we draw a slant going to left, upwards, crossing the vertical line opposite,

Then this line is brought as a slant downward crossing the vertical line on the right,

And again slanting upward, crossing both right & left vertical line,

Then we again go down towards the right side, crossing both vertical lines,

Then it goes slanting upward towards left.

Now, it touches the beginning point of left vertical line.

Then, we draw a dark pink curved line below this star.

This is how we draw a most powerful delination.

This is drawn in dark purple and dark pink colours.

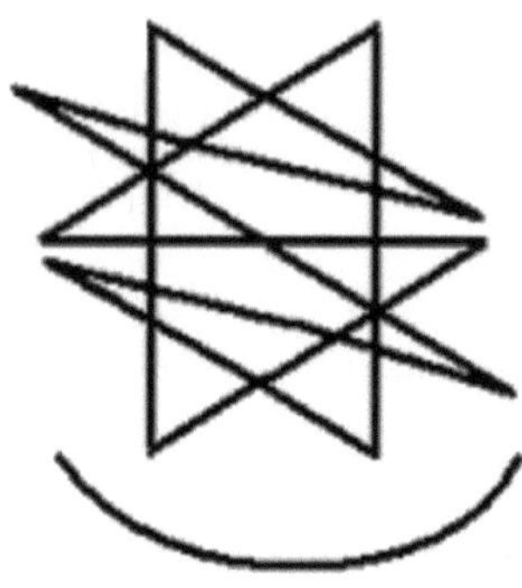

Adichi

The divine light drawn with the help of this delineation may be used in energizing intentions further.

This delination is useful in healing things much faster.

It has a power to intensify energies and sending them to right point faster and so on.

At other times, we give the divine light for general empowerment.

To use this, see the desired person/event in the energy field with all the other delineations.

To help anyone with the divine light, we draw this and send the field.

CHAPTER LIV

2. Detra - universal knowledge:

This delineation gets we connected with the universal knowledge.

To draw this delineation, we begin with a golden 'c'.

Then we draw a sleeping 'c' from lower point of first 'c',

then we draw tilted 'c open in left, starting from the end point of the second 'c',

Then we complete detra golden part by drawing another tilted 'c' open on right starting from the end point of the third 'c'.

We complete this fourth 'c' at the connecting point of first and second 'c's.

Now we draw a purple dot like small circle, in the centre of this formation.

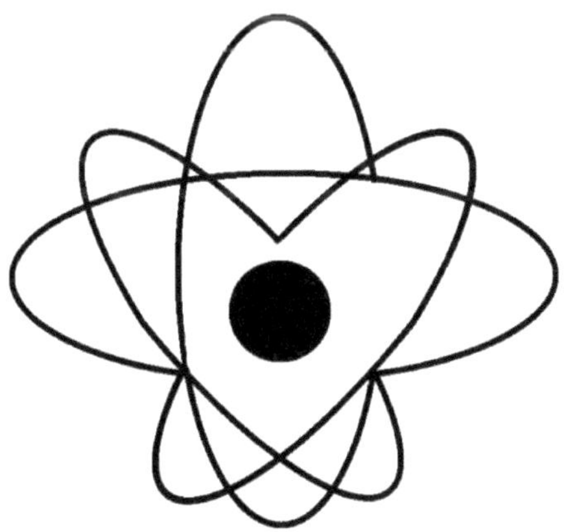

Detra

If we feel that we are not clear about the direction we must take, we may see ourselves in the energy field and draw this delineation and set the field around ourselves.

We will immediately get to know the right way of action.

We may do the same thing to other too if we wish that they get necessary knowledge, we can send this delineation to practically anyone to make him get the universal knowledge for some time.

CHAPTER LV

3. La Zen - divine help:

La Zen is a delineation that gets us divine help.

To draw this, we first draw a purple star,

This indicates the shine of the divine.

Then we draw a golden circle below it,

It represents the pure power of the divine.

Then we draw a dark pink 'A' below the golden circle.

Then we draw a vertical line that goes perpendicular to ground from the top point of 'A'.

Then we form an inverted triangle.

For this, we join the two points of the horizontal line of 'A' with bottom point of '|' inside 'A'.

Then we connect the bottom points of 'A' to the opposite points of the vertical line of 'A'.

This whole figure indicates a complete path of landing of the divine support with purest form of love and affection at every point.

Now we draw three golden circles below the three points at the bottom.

They indicate a firm presence of divine power that is supporting us in every venture we do.

This is how we get the complete figure of La Zen.

Of course, some may want to draw La zen in some other manner, and it is perfectly all right. This is because, the method of drawing this delination or rather any of the previous delinations is just narrated to make it easy for the seekers to mentally draw any of these delinations. But this is certainly not the hard and fast method of drawing it.

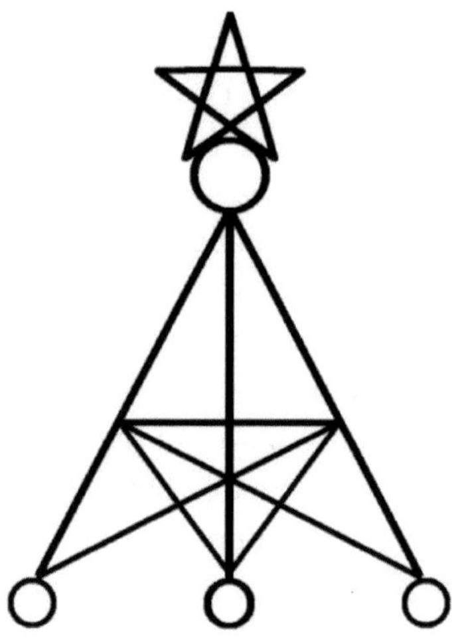

La Zen

This delineation is good to receive the divine help and divine intervention in matters which we feel we are not able to resolve with our existing capacity of energy work.

When we visualize the problem, or patient, we must first start visualizing that the problem is being dissolved or patient is being healed.

Then we must put this improving viion in energy field, desire the completion of problem solving or patient healing with divine help.

Then, we must draw the initial delinations and then, drawLa Zen, cover it with Polora and send the energy field to the existence.

With this, the divine masters intervene and extend their help to get the event of our choice or person we are going to heal, in right harmony.

CHAPTER LVI

4. Ta chi-awakening:

Ta chi is a delineation of awakening.

We draw a golden 'c' in the beginning.

Then we draw another golden small half circle with open part slanted down.

From the bottom point of first 'C',

we draw a curved purple '^' and a small purple horizontal line inside it.

Below it, we draw a blue diamond to complete drawing Ta Chi delineation.

Ta Chi

Awakening is necessary to make our thinking and understanding more powerful.

This can be achieved where understanding of events around is quite clear and one also gets the divine link between the events which apparently seem unconnected or out of harmony.

With awakening one can even adjust better with the surroundings. Also one can deal with life better and take better decisions.

To produce awakening, we may visualize the person/ group that we feel needs it in energy field, draw this and send the field.

CHAPTER LVII

5. Redizen-liberation:

Redizen is a delineation that represents liberation.

To draw this, we first draw a golden star.

Then we draw a curved purple '^' with purple horizontal line below it.

Then we draw two vertical lines below both the sides of '^' drawn below the two lines.

Then we draw a curved purple '^' with a purple horizontal line below each vertical line.

These curved purple '^' shapes intersect each other.

Then we draw three red lines below it, forming sleeping '7' figures with small line down.

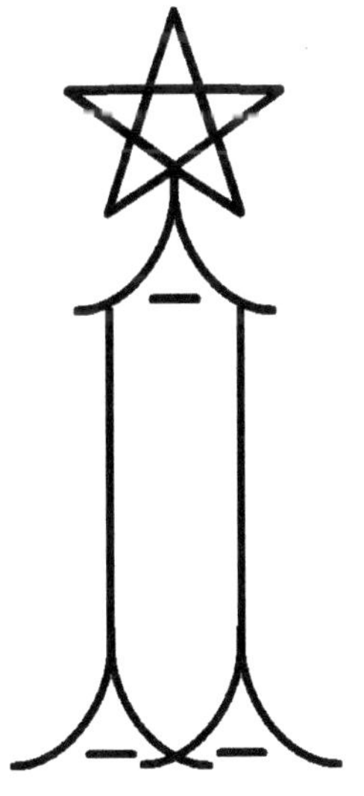

Redizen

Liberation does not just mean the Moksha that we get after the death.

It means being liberated from the issues that bind us and stop our growth.

Redizen helps us to get liberated from these issues and think and live freely without getting obstructed by them.

It is great to release the attachments that are not healthy.

Of course, healthy attachments never bind & obstruct.

If we wish to free someone from some attachment, even like any addiction or any other bad habits whom we want to be free from these thing, in the energy field and draw this delineation over the energy field to let it settle around the person seen in the energy field.

As we are doing this focus our attention on the binding issue so that the delineation will work specifically on it.

Of course if one wants one may even try to get actual Moksha by the repeated use of this delineation over ones own self!

These spiritual level delineations may work wonders when we use them after getting duly initiated.

With the other healing methods and earlier methods of Vishitao too, we may feel too limited at certain times to ger results in such occasions, we may use the spiritual level delineations of Vishitao.

Also with the attainment of this level, we may find that we are getting divine help and spiritual support with the use of other delineations too!

This means, now our work will automatically get help!

CHAPTER LVIII

Diagnosis & Scaning

Scanning is finding out what is the problem with a system; let it be physical body, or event or anything like machine.

As we scan something, we are trying to find out what is wrong with that thing or person or object. This is possible when we mentally see any object and try to know the area of its problem.

To do this we need to keep the eyes closed. Then we need to bring the thing that we want to scan in front of our eyes. As we do this, the problem is seen in a clear way.

First concentrate your mind.

Then think of the thing that you want to heal.

Now bring the image of that object in front of your eyes.

In the beginning close your eyes and imagine.

When you scan a person, begin with the head and go down looking for problem.

The Area with problem would be different from the rest of the body.

Make a note of it. Like this see the entire body of the patient from front and back.

After you finished ask the patient about his problems and see whether you were right.

Afterwards you can heal the patient.

You need to do this to a number of patients till the time you are perfect.

When you check an object for mechanical fault, the mechanism must be studied before you scan.

When you do this, you won't make errors in judgment.

You can then mentally study the entire machine and you'll know the area of problem quite easily which you may check with the expert again.

When you are checking an event, try to study all possible situations that create that event, only then start analyzing the event.

This would give you a greater insight into the event that you are working on.

With this insight, you will be in a better position to find out the exact cause of the problem.

You can practice scanning the persons, objects as well as events in this way.

When you do this, you need to feel energies with hands and must have your hands ready to feel these energies.

By practicing Vishitao regularly, one certainly gets this sensitivity, yet, there are some simple steps to make your hands sensitive to touch the aura and scan effectively.

These are:

1. Press the centre of your palms by thumb.
2. Press the fingers of both hands gently.
3. Rotate hands clockwise & counter clockwise.
4. Slowly increase distance between hands
5. Feel the pull
6. Your hands are ready to touch aura & scan.

In actual Vishitao training, this method os scanning and diagnosis is taught with practicals during the training of spiritual level of Vishitao.

When, How, From Whom, Why To Learn Vishitao

When:

One can learn all the four levels of Vishitao one by one, immediately one after the other, or with a gap between each two levels, as per convenience.

We announce Vishitao workshops from time to time.

They are either Offline at the decided venue, or online during the announced period.

Every year, 1st January, we certainly have either a one day offline Vishitao workshop, or we start an online vishitao workshop. So, seekers can keep a track for attending this workshop.

Readers can keep a track about the online training sessions on our site, https://multiversityofsuccess.in

What is a general duration of workshops:

Generally, Vishitao Basic level can be learned in one full day in offline training while it takes 10 sessions of 30 minutes in online training.

Vishitao Material level can be learned in Three full days in offline training while it takes 30 sessions of 30 minutes in online training.

Vishitao Mental level can be learned in Three full days in offline training while it takes 30 sessions of 30 minutes in online training.

Vishitao Spiritual levelcan be learned in Three full days in offline training while it takes 30 sessions of 30 minutes in online training.

How:

For attending the Vishitao workshop, one must register by calling or sending a whatsapp message on 7045862888.

After getting confirmation about the possibility of getting a seat in the workshop, one has to complete the registration by paying the fees to the same number using any online p0ayment mode.

How much do you pay:

The fees of Vishitao workshops for each level is different.

But there are times when for the benefit of seekers, some workshops are announced at discounted fees.

Also, Online workshops generally cost less because for them, venue ad logistics are not needed. Yet, online workshops take a long time, so, there is a risk of missing out some sessions.

From Whom:

Vishitao is presently taught only under a common roof of Multiversity of Success.

Vishitao is taught by its founder Dr. Rekhaa Kale, or by the Gurus trained and certified by her.

She has been training some masters as Vishitao Gurus and MahaGurus at various levels.

From time to time, she appoints some Vishitao Gurus to teach Vishitao at various levels of the workshop.

Yet, right now, to learn Vishitao, one has to register only by calling or sending message only to 7045862888.

Why to learn?

Benefits of learning Vishitao:

After this workshop, what one achieves is something that never happens in different types of separate individual or small group trainings of many other healing modalities....

Here, after the workshop, there is a follow up session, where one can share his experiences and also invite the patients whom one has healed during this period so that these patients can share their experiences.

Such follow-up sessions are helpful for the healers to develop greater confidence in healing different things and events, and also help them develop combinations of different techniques in order to produce speedy and powerful healing.

Then, one becomes a part of a Vishitao whatsapp group and interacts with all other vishitao healers who wish to be a part of that group.

One can also join the Vishitao FB page and share one's vishitao experiences over FB.

Also, whenever any seeker has any doubt or difficulty, the vishitao Guru's team is always ready to support that seeker all the time.

Applications Of Vishitao

Tips to combine delineations:

VISHITAO can be used effectively in all areas of life. This means practically for every purpose that we may have in life; we can use VISHITAO and get results! There are no limits for the function level of Vishitao. Only our visualization has to be clear and we must wish good for ourselves or others without harming anyone. Remember, the wrong doers are punished but not at our will. This is done with DIVINE WILL at a right time. So don't try to punish or harm anyone with Vishitao. We can use different combinations of delineations for different purposes in VISHITAO. Let us see possible combinations for various purposes:

A. Healing: End all healing with polora.

1= **Generalhealing**: Vishitao, kemizap, Reymzen

2= **Healing problems caused by cold**: Vishitao, kemizap, Reymzen, Grim

3= **Healing problems caused by heat**: Vishitao, kemizap, Reymzen, Sil

4= **Healing problems due to some growth:** Vishitao, kemizap, Reymzen, Melow

5= **Healing problems due to undergrowth**: Vishitao, kemizap, Reymzen, Megrow

6= **Healing problems due to disharmony:** Vishitao, kemizap, Reymzen, Chi hon Swe

7= **Healing problems due to depression:** Vishitao, kemizap, Reymzen, Megi

8= Healing lack of understanding: Vishitao, kemizap, Reymzen, Som, Ta Chi

9= Healing problems of black energies: Vishitao, kemizap, Reymzen, Kshed Swe

10= Healing absence of desire to get well: Vishitao, kemizap, Reymzen, Chi hon Swe, Swe

11= Healing relationships (Between two persons or groups): Vishitao, kemizap, Reymzen, O tu se

12= Healing relationships (By breaking wrong relations): Vishitao, kemizap, Reymzen, Kshed, Adhichi, La zen, Redizen, Swe, Chi hon Swe

13= Healing misunderstanding in families: Vishitao, kemizap, Reymzen, Awen, O tu se, La zen, Swe, Chi hon Swe, Stroc, Som

B. Creation: End all creation with HonSui.

1= Creating future event: Vishitao, kemizap, Metra, Swe, Adichi, Polora

2= Creating relationship: Vishitao, kemizap, Metra, O tu se, Swe, Adichi

3= Manifesting object: Vishitao, kemizap, Metra, Metiori, O ut se, Swe, Adhichi, Polora

4= Creating a protection shield: Vishitao, kemizap, Reymzen, Polora

5= Creating total harmony: Vishitao, kemizap, Metra, Chi hon Swe, Swe

6= Increase in some power etc: Vishitao, kemizap, Metra, Megrow, Swe

7= Decrease in some power, etc: Vishitao, kemizap, Metra, Melow, Swe

8= Creating abundance in life: Vishitao, kemizap, Metra, Ri me ga, Swe

Printed by Libri Plureos GmbH in Hamburg, Germany